Summit
Books

Into the Wood Chipper

A Whistleblower's Account of How the Trump Administration Shredded USAID

NICHOLAS ENRICH

SUMMIT BOOKS

New York   Amsterdam/Antwerp   London
Toronto   Sydney/Melbourne   New Delhi

Summit Books
An Imprint of Simon & Schuster, LLC
1230 Avenue of the Americas
New York, NY 10020

First Summit Books hardcover edition April 2026

Summit Books and colophon are registered trademarks of Simon & Schuster, LLC

Simon & Schuster strongly believes in freedom of expression and stands against censorship in all its forms. For more information, visit BooksBelong.com.

For information about special discounts for bulk purchases, please contact Simon & Schuster Special Sales at 1-866-506-1949 or business@simonandschuster.com.

The Simon & Schuster Speakers Bureau can bring authors to your live event. For more information or to book an event, contact the Simon & Schuster Speakers Bureau at 1-866-248-3049 or visit our website at www.simonspeakers.com.

Interior design by Carly Loman

Manufactured in the United States of America

1   3   5   7   9   10   8   6   4   2

Library of Congress Control Number has been applied for.

ISBN 978-1-6682-2695-7
ISBN 978-1-6682-2697-1 (ebook)

Scan here to get book recommendations, exclusive offers, and more delivered to your inbox.

To the public servants,
whose compassion, optimism, and devotion lift all of humanity

Do not obey in advance. Most of the power of authoritarianism is freely given. In times like these, individuals think ahead about what a more repressive government will want, and then offer themselves without being asked. A citizen who adapts in this way is teaching power what it can do.

— TIMOTHY SNYDER, *On Tyranny*

Contents

Foreword

By Atul Gawande

As I write this, it is a year after President Donald Trump ordered a ninety-day pause on the United States' foreign assistance for a reassessment of priorities as one of his first acts in office for his second term. At the time, those words came across to the American public as so bland as to seem almost meaningless. How harmful can a "pause" in anything really be? Reassessment seems like an appropriate thing for a new president to do. And what is meant by *foreign assistance*, anyway?

Within days, however, it became apparent that the order meant the immediate stoppage of the country's non-military aid abroad of every kind—in particular, the entire work of the United States Agency for International Development (USAID) from ending diseases like polio, tuberculosis, and HIV, to assisting with disaster relief in places such as Ukraine and Gaza, to protecting orphans, refugees, and religious minorities in some of the most hellish places on earth. Established in 1961, and championed by President John F. Kennedy, USAID had been created by Congress to provide sustained, expert support for the advancement of human survival, economies, and democracy in order to foster peace and stability and to counter the adversaries of freedom. There is no such thing as a temporary pause in such work. It soon became clear that hundreds of thousands would die.

But the new administration only doubled down, turning the pause into a wholesale dismantling of USAID. The toll since has been staggering. Boston University researchers have conservatively estimated that, one year later, the shutdown has already killed at least three-quarters of a million people, most of them children. The Institute for Health Metrics and Evaluation has projected the first increase in child deaths since the 1960s. Furthermore, with the entire infrastructure of the agency destroyed—more than ten thousand staff around the world were fired, programs touching hundreds of millions of lives were terminated, and networks and expertise built over six decades were lost—the bleeding is guaranteed to extend far into the future, even if funding and commitment to development assistance are restored. We are now witnessing what the historian Richard Rhodes termed "public man-made death," which, he asserted, has been perhaps the most overlooked cause of mortality in the last century.

Into the Wood Chipper is a remarkable, devastating insider account of exactly how this was able to occur. The agency was brought to its knees in a matter of a few weeks, despite being established in law. Nick Enrich was a civil servant at USAID during four administrations, two Democratic and two Republican, and as USAID's last acting head of global health, he was a witness to the pivotal events. He makes painfully clear that, in order to destroy the agency, people at the highest levels made choices to ignore the law, the procedures, and the harm to people's lives. Others—in Congress, the courts, and in the agency itself, including Nick—were then confronted with what they would do in the face of those choices. And what you encounter in his account of this tragedy is a Shakespearean range of human behavior and emotion: deceit, indifference to harm, bloodlust, thirst for power, incompetence, fear, accommodation, self-delusion, and, at all too few moments, courage.

From January 2022 to January 2025, I was USAID's assistant administrator for global health, a politically appointed and Senate-confirmed role. When I arrived, one of my primary concerns was how to manage bureaucrats. I'd absorbed all the stereotypes: they'd lack work ethic and talent and be impossible to hold accountable. I came to see that none of it was true.

Just weeks into my role, Russia launched missile attacks on Kyiv and a full-scale invasion of Ukraine, and I got a fast lesson in what USAID personnel were capable of. Among its many catastrophic effects, the war immediately cut off the country's medical supplies, shuttering pharmacies across Ukraine, and Russian cyberattacks disabled hospitals' digital systems. Inability to access medications and hospital care endangered vastly more lives than the bombs. For instance, a quarter million Ukrainians with HIV, and even more with diabetes and heart disease, depended on medicines for their lives. While the Bureau for Humanitarian Assistance was responsible for supporting the Ukrainian government's response for the millions of people suddenly displaced from their homes, my Bureau for Global Health was responsible for supporting the health system to remain functioning.

First, the foreign service staff in Kyiv focused on getting to safety. But within days of doing that, the health team had reconstituted in new locations, identified the supply chain and cybersecurity expertise they needed, and helped the government develop its strategy for keeping the health system going. Then, over the next several weeks, they helped the country execute, shifting hospital management systems to a new cloud-based system that was better protected against cyberattacks, working with the World Health Organization and numerous others to establish a new supply chain for medical supplies integrating more than five thousand humanitarian relief organizations, as well as getting six months of HIV medications mobilized for delivery. Within weeks, half the pharmacies in the country were supplied and open. Within three months, more than 80 percent were.

The personnel in D.C. and Eastern Europe had worked around the clock. They solved problems of every dimension. They followed the law. And they delivered at a scale and with an impact like I'd never experienced. During my time in office, that would prove to be my experience again and again.

Nick Enrich was a prime example of USAID's personnel. I'd recruited him from another bureau to serve, essentially, as the chief financial officer for our bureau, overseeing our processes for budgeting, planning, and program execution. This was a hot seat role. We ran a major international operation involving thousands of partner organizations and government entities in more than sixty-five countries. We dealt with problems that sometimes required planning in hours and delivering in days, but other times—when, say, working to strengthen outbreak surveillance systems around the world or to reduce global child deaths—required planning in months and delivering in years. We were constantly being called to account for our spending and outcomes by our congressional oversight committees.

On the one hand, USAID delivered arguably the highest impact per dollar of any agency in the U.S. government, saving lives by the millions with a global health budget in 2024 of just twenty-four dollars per American (out of fifteen thousand dollars per person paid in taxes). On the other hand, there were legitimate criticisms. The agency could be inefficient. It could foster dependency. Too much of its funding went to international institutions, rather than to local ones. I set improvement targets for each of these issues that I promised Congress we'd hit, and Nick was responsible for big parts of delivering on them. And deliver he did.

The Nick Enrich you encounter in these pages is the same Nick Enrich I knew from working together: a perceptive observer, a man with capacity to keep cool and perform under enormous pressure, and a patriot of the old-fashioned kind, motivated simply by the opportunity to serve and save lives. In his book, he writes the way he speaks and thinks—clearly, honestly, without euphemism or bureaucratese. He does not omit the details, including about his own regrets. This requires fearlessness.

When Trump's appointees arrived at USAID shortly after the inauguration—swinging their chainsaws, clueless about the agency's lifesaving work, and not actually interested in it—Nick was only at the midpoint of his career. He has still-young children at home and a mortgage to pay. He has no clear job ahead for his future. I have spoken to many former USAID staff who, to this day, will not speak publicly about what they saw and experienced, out of understandable fear of retaliation or being blacklisted from the few remaining jobs in their decimated field.

But not Nick. He blew the whistle as USAID was being dismantled and officially documented the inhumanity and illegality of the administration's actions. He filed an affidavit that was cited by the Supreme Court. And now his book exposes the people responsible and precisely how they precipitated public man-made death. He deserves our country's gratitude.

Author's Note

Conversations recounted in this book are drawn from contemporaneous notes and my best recollection of events. I have reproduced them as accurately as memory and verification allow. Quoted emails, directives, and other written communications come directly from original documents I retained. A collection of key documents is available at www.intothewoodchipper.com. I have not changed names or concealed identities, with the sole exception of a personal friend whose identity has no bearing on these events. I have excluded anything for which I lacked records or reliable notes.

There was far more I witnessed and could have documented. However, my access to USAID email and file systems was abruptly cut off in March 2025, limiting what I could corroborate. What follows is based exclusively on the evidence I was able to preserve. The rest will have to be told by others who had more time or foresight to retain records, or otherwise will wait until the government releases a full set.

The more than ten thousand people working at USAID on January 20, 2025 were employed through a wide array of hiring mechanisms: civil service, foreign service, foreign service nationals, institutional support contractors, personal service contractors, fellows, detailees, and others. I often refer to these groups collectively—*career officials, civil servants, staff members*—to distinguish them from political appointees and DOGE.

Although we served side by side in pursuit of USAID's mission, these employment categories carried real and sometimes painful differences. For example, when institutional support contractors were terminated in January, their pay and benefits ended immediately. Many exhausted unemployment benefits within weeks. By contrast, civil service officers like myself remained on paid administrative leave and later collected severance for months. These disparities shaped our individual experiences, though they represent just one dimension of the human consequences of the events described in this book.

Key Referenced Officials

(listed in alphabetical order)

Political Appointees

JOEL BORKERT: Acting chief of staff, USAID (Trump administration)

ATUL GAWANDE: Assistant administrator for global health, USAID (Biden administration)

MEGHAN HANSON: Director of policy, USAID (Trump administration)

KEN JACKSON: Acting deputy administrator January 21 to February 3, then acting deputy administrator for management and resources and "senior bureau official" starting February 3, USAID (Trump administration)

ADAM KORZENIEWSKI: USAID White House liaison (Trump administration)

MARK LLOYD: Assistant to the administrator for conflict prevention and stabilization, USAID (Trump administration)

PETER MAROCCO: State Department director of foreign assistance, and acting deputy administrator of USAID starting February 3 (Trump administration)

TIMOTHY MEISBURGER: Assistant to the administrator for humanitarian assistance, USAID (Trump administration)

SAMANTHA POWER: Administrator, USAID (Biden administration)

LAKEN RAPIER: Senior advisor for communications, USAID (Trump administration)

MARCO RUBIO: Secretary of State, and acting administrator of USAID starting February 3 (Trump administration)

RUSSELL VOUGHT: Director, White House Office of Management and Budget (Trump administration)

CARTWRIGHT WEILAND: USAID transition landing team lead (Trump administration)

Department of Government Efficiency (DOGE)

EDWARD CORISTINE: USAID DOGE team member

CLAYTON CROMER: USAID DOGE team member

LUKE FARRITOR: USAID DOGE team member

GAVIN KLIGER: USAID DOGE team member

JEREMY LEWIN: USAID DOGE team lead

ELON MUSK: Head of DOGE

USAID Career Staff

TRAVIS BETZ: Outbreak Response Team lead, Office of Infectious Diseases, Bureau for Global Health

CARMEN COLES: Deputy assistant administrator for global health (on administrative leave from January 27 to February 9)

NICHOLAS ENRICH: Director, Office of Policy, Programs, and Planning, Bureau for Global Health, then acting assistant administrator for global health

MEGAN FOTHERINGHAM: Deputy director, Office of Infectious Diseases, Bureau for Global Health

BRIAN FRANTZ: Acting assistant administrator for Africa

RAMONA GODBOLE: Deputy director, Office of Policy, Programs, and Planning, Bureau for Global Health

NICHOLAS GOTTLIEB: Director of employee and labor relations, Office of Human Capital and Talent Management

JASON GRAY: Acting administrator of USAID, then chief information officer

ALYSSA JERNIGAN: Budget director, Office of Policy, Programs, and Planning, Bureau for Global Health

HAN KANG: Deputy assistant administrator for global health (on administrative leave from January 27 to February 9)

NATALIA MACHUCA: Deputy director, Office of Professional Development and Management Support, Bureau for Global Health

BRIAN MCGILL: Deputy director of security

NIDA PARKS: Chief of staff, Bureau for Global Health

JAMI RODGERS: Director, Office of Acquisition and Assistance, and senior procurement officer, Bureau for Management

PAUL SEONG: Foreign service officer, senior advisor, Office of the Administrator

NADEEM SHAH: Deputy director, Office of Acquisition and Assistance, Bureau for Management

JOHN VOORHEES: Director of security

JULIE WALLACE: Senior deputy assistant administrator for global health (on administrative leave from January 27 to February 9)

Prologue

It was a cold Thursday evening in February 2025, exactly one month into the Trump administration. It already felt like it had been years. I was sitting in the loud, dingy basement of Astro Beer Hall in downtown Washington with three of my colleagues from the U.S. Agency for International Development. We had claimed a small table in the corner of the bar, squeezed between a birthday party and a corporate happy hour. It had been another wretched day, and I didn't know how much longer we could keep this up.

Our agency was facing an extinction event. The meteor had already hit, and USAID, which for more than sixty years had saved millions of lives around the world from disease and poverty, had been left smoldering in ruins.

It had started on Inauguration Day, when President Donald Trump signed an executive order pausing all foreign assistance. Things had unraveled from there. Elon Musk, the tech billionaire and social media tycoon, had set out to destroy the agency, having seized on USAID as a test case to demonstrate the power of the Department of Government Efficiency, or DOGE, his new quasi-governmental creation. He didn't know what USAID did, or why it existed in the first place, and he didn't seem to care. All he knew was that he intended to feed USAID, in his words, "into the wood chipper."

Musk's operatives had put the agency's leadership on administrative leave and had summarily fired thousands of international development experts in Washington and across the globe. In a half-hearted effort to stave off a humanitarian catastrophe, the new U.S. secretary of state, Marco Rubio, issued a waiver that supposedly allowed USAID to resume its life-saving work. But Trump's appointees and Musk's DOGE team ignored the waiver. Even as the administration publicly claimed that lifesaving programs were continuing, behind closed doors they forged ahead on their single-minded mission to destroy USAID. Funding was frozen. The workforce was slashed. Systems crumbled. Contracts were terminated. They even removed USAID's name from the entrance to its headquarters in the Ronald Reagan federal office building on Pennsylvania Avenue.

The results were rapid, predictable, and catastrophic. In Zambia, pregnant women with HIV could no longer find medicine to prevent their babies from being infected. In Sierra Leone, crates of donated drugs sat expiring on warehouse shelves instead of saving children's lives. In war-torn Sudan, malnourished families walked all day to communal kitchens, only to find them closed.

During this whirlwind of destruction, I had been promoted, without warning, to the top position in USAID's Bureau for Global Health, where I was ordered to endorse the termination of these programs and the firing of hundreds of my colleagues. This was not what I had signed up for.

My distress had intensified as I watched Musk flagrantly lie. Standing next to Trump in the Oval Office, he assured the gathered journalists and their live TV audiences that USAID's programs to prevent the spread of deadly diseases like Ebola and HIV were still operating. They weren't. DOGE was dismantling them piece by piece. At the same time, Secretary Rubio and his team were blaming me and my colleagues for the undeniable and deadly mess, accusing us of intentionally creating bureaucratic hurdles to block delivery of food and medicine. Rubio called USAID's career staff "completely uncooperative" and "insubordinate," even as his own political team stonewalled our desperate efforts to restart lifesaving aid. Trump then piled on, claiming that USAID was run by "radical lunatics" and pushing absurd lies about our work.

By late February, all hope of preserving even a fraction of USAID's work seemed lost. The Bureau for Global Health, originally nearly eight hundred people strong, was on the verge of being reduced to a staff measured in two digits, and none of our programs were operative.

And so on this Thursday evening I found myself at Astro Beer Hall with Ramona Godbole, Nida Parks, and Natalia Machuca, three of my senior colleagues, who had been on the front lines with me for the past weeks, as we tried—over and over—to blunt the effects of the staff cuts, funding freezes, and contract terminations.

I was exhausted, running on fumes. I had slept no more than an hour the previous night. My team and I had been up late working yet another unsolvable problem the agency's political leaders had manufactured for us. It was just the latest in a month of self-inflicted chaos that comes along with political appointees who have no understanding of or interest in learning the rules or laws of government.

We were trying to respond to a deadly Ebola outbreak in Uganda, had been trying for weeks. But we had been stymied at every turn. The night before, USAID's leaders finally agreed to our plan to send twenty-seven thousand sets of personal protective equipment into the outbreak zone— except there was a catch. They wouldn't authorize payment to release the PPE from the Kenyan warehouse where it was being stored. Instead, they had ordered me to go get the supplies myself. I had tried to explain that was not how we operate. Even if I could get there, and had a license to drive a truck, I was not authorized to transport the PPE across the Ugandan border. Besides, sending me to do all this would cost more than the nominal transfer fee (we had already paid for the PPE, we just needed to move it). This was why USAID contracts for this type of service, I explained.

But my new bosses were not convinced. They insisted that I go pick it up and make the delivery. Oh, and one more thing: They gave me twelve hours to get it done.

That order had come just before 8 p.m., and my team and I had been flailing to find some way to move the supplies ever since. The twelve-hour deadline had come and gone, and I hadn't been fired yet, at least as far as I knew. More important, we were no closer to providing the needed PPE to respond to the Ebola outbreak.

I can't take much more of this, I thought. Ramona must have been able to read it on my face, and she was at least as fed up as I was.

"We have to get the fuck out!" she blurted, taking a swig from her wineglass. Normally soft-spoken and careful with her words, Ramona had reached her breaking point. I knew she was right, but it was hard to hear. Resigning from our jobs would mean giving up on everything: our careers, our mission, the lives that depended on our work. This was not the first time Ramona had argued that this was our only option; she had drafted a resignation letter two weeks earlier, and I had nearly signed on to it several times. Each time, I had wavered, thinking that we could do more good if we stayed in our jobs and fought the administration's onslaught from the inside.

Nida had always argued against Ramona's drastic remedy. Once again she made her case. "We *cannot* quit yet," she said. "Not while there's still a sliver of hope we can restart something. I know we're driving ourselves insane and making zero progress, but as long as there is anything left we can do, we have to keep trying."

"But what are we actually doing?" asked Natalia. "Can you name one thing we've done since this administration came in that you're proud of? Because I can't."

I tried to think of an answer, but nothing came. That was a bad sign. I had worked at USAID for more than twelve years, and it was rare to go even a day without feeling proud of what I was doing. I was now the agency's top global health official, but my dream job had turned into a nightmare. Day by day, at the direction of our reckless and vindictive political leadership, we were abandoning our lifesaving programs and the people who relied on them, disbanding our staff, shredding our agency from within. We were digging graves—our own, and those for millions of others.

I drained my beer and headed to the bar for another round. Three more pilsners and another glass of the happy hour red. Threading my way back through the crowd with the four precariously balanced drinks, I took stock of our situation. I was coming around to Ramona's point of view.

Back at the table, I slid the drinks to my colleagues, wondering how we—just four civil servants—could find a way to get the truth out, in the face of lies from the world's richest man and from the highest-ranking officials in the Trump administration. Ramona, Nida, and Natalia had been huddled together conspiratorially while I competed for the bartender's attention. Now they went silent as I returned. All eyes were on me.

Even in the bar's dim light, I noticed Ramona's sly smile. "We don't have to go down quietly," she said. "We could blaze out."

Natalia nodded in agreement. Ramona went on: "Nick, you're the highest-ranking global health official at USAID. If you tell the world what they've done—how many lives it'll cost, how it'll make the U.S. more vulnerable to the next pandemic—people will listen. Maybe Congress would even act."

The idea was intoxicating. I didn't want the political appointees at USAID to get away with the cruelty they'd shown as they tore down decades of progress in global health. I wanted to expose their indifference and ignorance, which was already costing lives, and it was going to get so much worse.

"Would anyone even believe me?" I asked.

"If we do it right, they'd have to," Natalia jumped in. "We've got the records. Every email, every document, all the notes. What if we wrote it up? Every illegal order, every time they stopped us from saving lives, every time we warned them and they shrugged us off. I'd love to write one last great memo." Left unsaid was the obvious next step: That memo and evidence would have to be leaked far and wide.

My colleagues were serious, and now I was intrigued. At what point was it time to take a stand? When would it be too late to speak up?

"What do you think, Nida?" I asked. She was the least ready to give up the fight, and she had talked me off the ledge a few times already when I had been prepared to quit. But Ramona and Natalia were not proposing surrender. Far from it. "Do you think we should blaze out, too?"

She hesitated. "We're definitely running out of other options," she said finally. "At least it would be a warning for other agencies, the ones they'll come for next."

Nida was right. This wasn't just about USAID. We were the first victim of DOGE's chainsaw, but we certainly would not be the last. The staff at whichever agency was fed through the wood chipper next—the Consumer Financial Protection Bureau, or the Centers for Disease Control and Prevention, or the Department of Education—could learn from what had happened to us at USAID and avoid some of our mistakes. The alternative looked untenable. If we kept our heads down, quietly carrying out the administration's dangerous and unethical orders, weren't we just helping them expand their assault to other federal programs? If we didn't speak up, who would?

I looked around the table: Together the four of us had spent fifty-five years at USAID. What would it mean to walk away from that? Where would we go from here?

In the dark corner of the bar, I tried to grasp how much ground had been lost. In a single month, I had gone from being a stalwart civil servant, dutifully carrying out the president's foreign assistance agenda, to a potential whistleblower, ready to expose the administration's lies, its cruelty, and the danger its actions posed to U.S. national security.

I thought of all my colleagues at USAID. As the walls closed in, they, too, faced terrible choices.

Now the choice was mine.

PART ONE

STORM CLOUDS

1.

A Key Strategic Instrument

At eight o'clock on an unseasonably warm November morning in 2024, I walked into the seventh-floor conference room of the USAID Annex building. Atul Gawande, the assistant administrator for global health, had called an emergency meeting with his leadership team. Our small group—Atul's four deputies, his chief medical officer, his chief of staff, and me, the director of policy, programs, and planning—took our seats overlooking L'Enfant Plaza in Southwest Washington, D.C., and waited for Atul to join us. On any other morning, this normally jovial group would have used the extra time before Atul convened the meeting to iron out the details of a pressing issue, to quickly debrief a recent conference or site visit, or to recap a kid's swim meet. But on this morning, Wednesday, November 6, no one uttered a word.

A minute later, Atul entered the room, his usually loping gait truncated to a subdued shuffle. President Biden's appointee to lead global health for USAID sat down and told us why he had called us in: He wanted to discuss what had happened the night before and what it might mean for USAID. Donald Trump had won the 2024 presidential election just a few hours earlier. This was not 2016; no one was shocked by the outcome. But Atul was deftly attuned to staff morale. He wanted to address the anxiety that many of USAID's civil servants were doubtless experiencing now that Trump's victory was a reality.

Tall, confident, and always fashionably dressed, Atul could come across as intimidating in meetings. It was partly his intelligence, which came through quickly in his pointed questions. But he was also inquisitive; though he was not lacking for his own ideas, he was always trying to improve them. He would fix you with a deep stare and probe for your recommendation, trying to make sure he understood all angles before making a decision. And on that Wednesday morning, he knew he needed to walk a fine line as he considered how to talk to the staff about Trump's election.

All presidential elections loom large in the minds of federal employees. The outcome determines who our bosses will be for the next four years, as well as the policies that we will be implementing. But in spite of its central importance to our daily lives, we almost never talk about elections at work. The civil service is prohibited from engaging in politics; the Hatch Act specifically bars federal employees from discussing, promoting, or participating in political activities or campaigns while at work, to ensure the nonpartisan administration of federal programs. Believe it or not, the vast majority of federal workers that I've encountered take this seriously. Still, you didn't need explicit workplace conversations to realize that many federal employees were afraid of what a second Trump presidency might mean.

For the first time, an incoming administration was going far beyond expressing disagreement with federal policies. Trump's team had identified the civil service—which implements the policies of all presidents, regardless of political party—as the enemy. Rather than being relied on for our expertise and institutional knowledge to implement the new president's priorities, we faced the distinct possibility that President-elect Trump wanted to get rid of us entirely. Russell Vought, the incoming director of the White House Office of Management and Budget, made no secret of his planned assault on the federal workforce: "We want the bureaucrats to be traumatically affected," he said. "When they wake up in the morning, we want them to not want to go to work, because they are increasingly viewed as the villains. We want their funding to be shut down." In case that wasn't clear, Vought added: "We want to put them in trauma."

To be characterized as villains by the man who was in some ways our new boss was concerning. Now that Trump had won, it was impossible not to wonder what it might be like to work for someone whose stated goal was to dissuade his employees from wanting to come to work. As civil servants, our job was to implement the policies of the administration. Were we going to be asked to traumatize ourselves?

Atul summoned us that morning so that we could figure out how to talk to our teams about our troubling new circumstances. True to form, he had already prepared a communications proposal. He suggested two primary talking points:

1. There are many unknowns. Although there will be lots of questions, we have very few answers, and we don't know what we don't know. Spreading rumors and speculation on what may be coming will be counterproductive.
2. The Trump administration knows the value of USAID's work. We have been here before, during Trump's previous term, and, despite some policy differences, they supported most of our global health investments. While politics plays a role at the margins, the value of our work in global health is indisputable and nonpartisan.

At the recommendation of Julie Wallace, Atul's top deputy—USAID's highest-ranking civil servant in global health—we added a third point:

3. Everyone is entitled to their feelings about the election, but ultimately our job is to prepare the next administration to effectively implement their priorities, whether or not we agree with them on a personal level.

Atul wanted us to reach consensus in part because it would be us, not him, doing much of the communicating in the weeks ahead. As a Democratic political appointee, his days at USAID were numbered. And given Atul's stature, that was going to represent a body blow. A former *New Yorker* staff writer and a renowned surgeon, Atul had led the Bureau for Global Health (GH) with an unusual blend of technical expertise and storytelling prowess. Not only did he believe in USAID's mission, he helped us articulate it. He insisted that all our work should be linked to well-defined objectives and expected results so that it was clear how our tuberculosis interventions, for example, fed into our overall global health strategy. He pressed us to deprioritize any activities that were not aligned. Now his tenure was nearing its end.

As our meeting wrapped up, Atul reminded us to not let our people lose sight of everything USAID had accomplished, and everything we still needed to do.

Until recently, most Americans had never even heard of USAID. Before the 2024 election, people looked at me with a blank stare when I told them where I worked. I had friends and family members who, for the twelve years I worked there, had no idea what USAID was, or what I did. One of my closest friends, a former college roommate, would insist that I worked for the State Department, failing to grasp that USAID was a separate agency, despite my having described the job to him a dozen times.

Did Americans understand that our government did good things around the world? That we responded to disease outbreaks, conflicts, and natural disasters, and that we provided food to alleviate famines? That we taught children to read where literacy rates were low and supported women-owned businesses to bolster fragile economies? Perhaps. But I think most would be shocked to learn the scale of USAID's services and impact.

It starts with a number: 92 million. That is how many deaths USAID prevented over the past two decades, according to a recent study published in *The Lancet*, a leading medical journal. That number brings me great pride. Not as an employee of USAID, where I worked for many of those years, but as an American. If you are an American, I hope it brings you pride, too. It is a reflection of the fact that our society decided that the official policy of our country should be for all of us to chip in a little bit to save and improve the lives of millions and millions of people. And all it cost was an average of $24 a year per American.

Ninety-two million, and we were just getting started. Several USAID investments in new drugs, vaccines, and technological innovations had us right at the cusp of achieving a world free from fear of some of the deadliest diseases of the past century: malaria, HIV, and tuberculosis. Our plans for 2025 included rolling out the first malaria vaccines ever approved for widespread use; a game-changing HIV prevention drug, lenacapavir, one of the most promising breakthroughs in HIV prevention in decades; and expanding the use of AI-powered testing tools to prevent the spread of tuberculosis.

But maybe you don't care about what happens overseas. You care about the United States. It's not crazy to think that American tax dollars should be spent in America, which has plenty of its own problems to worry about. That is the beauty of USAID's work. It benefits Americans. Tuberculosis and HIV don't stop at international borders. Neither do other infectious diseases, as we all know having recently endured a global pandemic. Even if you're not convinced of the value of goodwill and partnership built through decades of American generosity, USAID's work to enable countries' health systems to detect outbreaks before they spread makes us safer here at home. And people who live in poverty in far-off countries might not immediately seem like America's problem. But improving healthcare access is proven to alleviate migration and conflict, saving Americans from needing to resort to much more costly interventions. Our foreign assistance investments have paid off in long-standing economic benefits, too. Several countries that were former aid recipients have since developed into major American trading partners, including South Korea, Taiwan, Chile, and Brazil.

This is not a new revelation. For decades, the United States has demonstrated that investment in international development is a down payment on our own security. The recognition that America's strength and prosperity depended on conditions beyond our borders was forged at a volatile moment, when the world's dangers pressed closer than ever.

In March 1961, Fowler Hamilton sat nervously in a small office in the West Wing of the White House. Down the corridor, plans were being finalized for the Bay of Pigs invasion of Cuba, which would fail spectacularly in less than a month, but Hamilton was oblivious to the comings and goings of the nation's top military strategists as they streamed by his door.

A Wall Street lawyer turned international development policy expert, Hamilton was hunched over a draft of what would become the Foreign Assistance Act of 1961. He had been tapped by President John F. Kennedy to consolidate dozens of overlapping Cold War aid programs into a single, streamlined agency that could wield international development as a weapon of influence and peace.

As an added challenge, Hamilton had been tasked to do this alone, in secrecy. Kennedy insisted on the establishment of an independent agency, freed from the tangled knot of the State Department's bureaucracy, to advance international development as a primary pillar of U.S. foreign policy rather than an afterthought. Yet among the upper echelons of the State Department there was a deep mistrust of Hamilton, who was seen as a foreign policy outsider, imprudently empowered by Kennedy to remove a substantial part of the department's portfolio—foreign aid—from their control. They had no intention of ceding their authority to a newly created agency, and so Hamilton was forced to work on his own, outside official channels.

When his blueprint for a single federal agency devoted to foreign aid arrived in Congress, it faced immediate skepticism. Southern Democrats worried it would send too much money abroad. Conservative Republicans feared a creeping global welfare state. Even some within Kennedy's inner circle doubted whether a centralized international aid agency could deliver results without becoming another sprawling Washington bureaucracy.

Yet Kennedy pushed ahead, challenging legislators to make the 1960s the "Decade of Development" and calling for the establishment of a new Agency for International Development to carry out this mission.

Kennedy understood the stakes. The Soviet Union was pouring billions into infrastructure and technical support for newly independent nations across the globe. Washington needed to provide a counterweight to the Soviet outreach by offering a rival ideology and credible partnership to countries around the world. "Unless we begin to identify ourselves not only with the anti-communist fight, but also with the fight against poverty and hunger," Kennedy argued, "these people are going to begin to turn to the communists as an example."

On August 31, 1961, after months of bruising negotiations on Capitol Hill, Congress passed the Foreign Assistance Act, and Kennedy signed it into law on September 4. That November, he issued Executive Order 10973, officially creating the U.S. Agency for International Development. Fowler Hamilton was appointed as USAID's first administrator. A new era of U.S. international development had begun.

The creation of USAID reflected a belief that foreign aid could serve as both a key strategic instrument of U.S. foreign policy and a force for improving lives around the world. Charged with advancing global development and providing humanitarian assistance in ways that promote democratic values and U.S. national security, the agency helped low- and middle-income countries build the capacity for self-sustained progress and to ultimately reduce dependence on aid. USAID worked across sectors ranging from global health and education to food security, energy, governance, and disaster response, partnering with governments, civil society, and multilateral institutions like the United Nations. USAID exemplified American soft power by fostering goodwill and strengthening alliances where military or economic influence alone might have come up short, projecting U.S. interests and ideals through cooperation rather than coercion.

President Barack Obama put it best: "To many people around the world, USAID *is* the United States." Certainly, USAID has been the primary lifeline for recipients of international aid. Delivering 43 percent of all government funding for health aid around the world, USAID was the leading force for increasing global life expectancy and improving health and well-being.

Yet USAID was relatively tiny. Our approximately ten thousand employees made up less than 0.3 percent of the nonmilitary federal workforce, and the agency's $40 billion annual appropriation (of which less than $2 billion was for administrative costs) was only 0.7 percent of the federal budget. Depending on how you measure it, USAID was approximately the twentieth largest agency in the government. Good luck naming all nineteen above it, I know I can't. We didn't sell weapons systems, we didn't build bridges to nowhere, and we didn't make you take off your shoes at the airport. You would be entirely forgiven if you had never even heard of USAID before President Trump's second term.

Although USAID mostly flew under the radar, as 2025 approached we began to step up our efforts to make sure that the incoming administration was clear on what the agency did and why it was important. It was one thing for my college roommate to be clueless, but we needed our new bosses to be well-versed on our programs and their value.

The transfer of power from one administration to the next is perhaps the most sacred of all traditions in American government. The pageantry of the Inauguration Day celebration is a carefully scripted and unmistakable symbol that in the United States, democracy, and no individual, is king. But behind the scene that unfolds every fourth January at the West Front of the Capitol, a far less glamorous but equally important transition takes place in the months preceding the public ceremony. To little fanfare, the civil service prepares for the change in administration. Each federal agency executes a well-defined process to inform the incoming administration about what the agency does and how it operates, so that the new president's team will be able to hit the ground running on January 20.

The transition process does not depend on the good graces of the outgoing administration; it is defined by law in the Presidential Transition Act, which specifies the actions that must be implemented whenever a new president comes into office and defines the materials that must be prepared for the new administration's landing team. The transition process is entirely nonpartisan; the political appointees of the outgoing administration are not allowed to be involved. Since the process starts before the election (the new landing team may arrive as early as the day after the election—there can even be two landing teams if the winner has not yet been determined), we don't even know whether our audience will be Republicans or Democrats. Our incentives are clear: We want the incoming team to immediately recognize our excellence and expertise, the value of our work. The landing team represents the president-elect, who was chosen by the American people to lead the executive branch. The job of a civil servant is to help him do so.

Trump's inauguration would mark the fourth administration I had worked for, two Republican and two Democratic, so I was no stranger to the process.

At USAID, like all other federal agencies, we establish a transition team at headquarters to brief the new arrivals, show them around the office, and answer their questions. It's sort of like Take Your Child to Work Day except it's your new boss instead of your child. And you really need them to pay attention, because they're planning a lot of changes. It is critical that they understand how things work, ideally so that they can effectively steer the agency in a positive direction. Or at least so they don't mess things up too badly.

While USAID was staffed primarily by career officials who remained in their positions from one administration to the next, the agency's leadership is composed of political appointees who are replaced every four or eight years. USAID was led by an administrator who was appointed by the president and confirmed by the Senate. The administrator was supported by a small executive team, which included a chief of staff, deputy administrators, general counsel, chief financial officer, chief information officer, and a few others—a mix of political appointees and career civil servants. Outside the administrator's office, the agency's headquarters was divided into several bureaus, each of which was led by an assistant administrator, a political appointee who, with a few exceptions, was also confirmed by the Senate.

GH, for example, is what we called a "pillar bureau" that focused on a specific development sector—global health—and Atul Gawande was Biden's appointee as assistant administrator for GH. Other pillar bureaus covered other sectors, like food security, the environment, humanitarian response, economic development, human rights, and governance. In addition to the pillar bureaus, "central bureaus" were responsible for operations like budget, policy, human resources, and contract management. Finally, "regional bureaus" were just what they sound like, each responsible for a region of the world where USAID works. Each bureau was led by a new political appointee following a presidential transition.

The political appointees were based at USAID headquarters, but most of the work happened overseas. The majority of USAID's workforce was stationed at USAID missions located in the more than one hundred countries where we operated, working in tandem with host governments to implement our programs. Led by American foreign service officers who rotated their posting every few years, the permanent staff at missions were primarily locally hired employees, called foreign service nationals, with expertise in the various development work we ran in each country. Of course, the policy decisions made at headquarters drive the nature of our programs around the world, so the pressure was high on our Washington-based team to initiate a successful transition.

Of the three presidential transitions during my career, however, none were normal. Four years earlier, in the chaos following the 2020 election, President Trump's General Services Administration refused to authorize the commencement of the presidential transition process. In turn, the acting head of USAID, John Barsa, refused to cooperate with the Biden landing team, denying access to agency facilities, systems, and staff. Although they ultimately gained access once the GSA eventually granted authorization, the landing team was delayed by several weeks.

Four years before that was even weirder: There was no landing team at all following the 2016 election. There we sat, briefing books at the ready, for someone, anyone, from the incoming Trump administration to visit USAID and learn about what we do. But they never showed up. We went uneasily about our business for more than six months into Trump's presidency, wondering if they had forgotten about us, until we were finally joined by our new administrator, Mark Green, in August 2017.

In the days immediately following the 2024 election, we were once again ready to meet our new bosses, anxious to bring them up to speed. We knew they would have tough questions about and potentially even animosity toward some of our programs, but we were prepared to explain and defend our work. Ultimately, our new priorities would be determined by the incoming political leadership, but we had high hopes that they would analyze the data we'd be providing them to inform their decisions.

In hindsight, that might seem naive. At the time, though, it made sense. The hostile rhetoric from Trump and his team portraying public servants as lazy or conniving seemed to be just that: rhetoric. Fighting deadly diseases, expanding access to quality healthcare, and increasing global life expectancy were goals that had been authorized by Congress and had remained priorities for decades, across Democratic and Republican administrations. It didn't occur to me that they would now be in jeopardy.

2

Long Trek

Around 7 p.m. on Tuesday, November 26, 2024, as I rode my bike into the driveway, my wife, Jordanna, pulled up behind me in our minivan. The sun had set two hours earlier, and the blinding headlights bore into me like a criminal suspect sitting in an interrogation room. In a flash, I realized why I was feeling guilty: I had completely forgotten it was my night to drive our daughter, Hazel, to soccer practice.

Jordanna stepped out of the car and cut me off before I could sneak in an apology.

"Don't worry, I took her," she said. "When you weren't home by six thirty, I had a feeling something came up at work. Everything okay?"

It was not the first time since the election that I had been distracted by a work crisis and shirked my responsibilities at home. Nor, I had a sinking feeling, would it be the last.

"I'm really sorry," I said.

As we walked into the house, I knew I was lucky to have her. It wasn't just that Jordanna had picked up my slack (again), saving our nine-year-old daughter from being late to soccer practice (last week it had been Zander, our eleven-year-old son, whom I had failed to retrieve from his Hebrew lesson). Jordanna, a director at a Washington-based nonprofit organization, somehow never seemed to have any problems balancing her work with Hazel's ever-changing soccer schedule—or, for that matter, with Zander's schedule, or the parent-teacher organizations, or the frenetic social calendar she kept for both of us, which this week included hosting Thanksgiving dinner for seventeen guests. Problem-solving was embedded in her DNA; I could tell her about my issue at work, and she would patiently listen and help me solve it.

Today's problem was the latest rumor that Congress was planning to place a hold on USAID's access to funding, an attempt to run out the clock on our ability to implement our programs during the waning months of President Biden's term. Actually, the rumor was only part of the problem. The immediate issue was the response that Samantha Power, USAID's outgoing administrator, was proposing: To defiantly use the funds, even if Congress was trying to hold them.

My assignment—the one that had distracted me from remembering to drive to soccer practice—had landed that afternoon: devise a timeline to satisfy all procedural and legal requirements on the funds so that, if negotiations with Congress stalled, there would still be time to spend the money before Inauguration Day. The plan was aggressive, but Power and the other Biden appointees at USAID did not have much to lose; they would be out the door in less than two months. For them, completing their priorities was more urgent than ever, and anything that was not finalized by January 20 would be left for the Trump team to decide how to proceed. In global health, this meant millions of dollars planned for programs that Trump was not likely to support, including for USAID's partnership with the World Health Organization to monitor diseases globally, update clinical guidance, and authorize new drugs, and for family planning and reproductive health programs that protected the health, lives, and livelihoods of millions of women and girls.

It was completely reasonable for Power to want to push through funding for these critical programs, but she wouldn't be the one who would have to face the blowback from the next Congress. Moving the funds over the objections of the congressional committees that oversee foreign aid was risky. We would be jeopardizing our longer-term priorities, which required congressional support, just to move funds in the short term based solely on speculation that President-elect Trump might try to claw back unspent money once he took office. We didn't know for sure that Trump would do that or even if he could. After all, Congress had already appropriated the funds, by law, to USAID for specific purposes, and the Trump administration would be bound, as the Biden administration had been, to use the money as directed. On the other hand, our highest legislative priorities for global health were potentially at stake. Over the next year, we were going to need Congress to continue funding global health programs, and particularly to protect recent investments we had made in global health security in fifty countries. We also needed Congress's support for the reauthorization of PEPFAR, the U.S. government's flagship initiative to combat HIV, the future of which was in doubt for the first time since its enactment more than twenty years earlier. Pissing off Congress now felt like a bad idea.

"Is it legal?" Jordanna asked, cutting off my rant and getting right to the point. "Are you allowed to spend the funds even if Congress told you to hold?" I explained that, yes, technically it was allowed, although it had only been done on rare occasions. Congressional holds were generally respected by the executive branch as a matter of professional courtesy, but there was no legal barrier to using the funds. After all, the funds had already been appropriated for USAID's use.

"So, then, what is the issue?" she went on. "It's legal, and it's a political decision." The subtext: It wasn't my call. The politicos had made the decision, I'd pointed out the possible downsides, and they were sticking with the plan.

She was right, of course. My job as a civil servant was to implement, not to set policy. That means sometimes doing things that conflict with my own priorities. My role was to provide advice and expertise on how best to execute, but the decision was theirs. It was as simple as that.

Rewind two decades.

At 2:20 p.m. on May 27, 2003, President George W. Bush sat at a small desk on the stage of the Dean Acheson Auditorium in the State Department headquarters building, flanked by an array of world leaders and foreign policy advisors. He picked up a pen and scrawled his signature onto the U.S. Leadership Against HIV/AIDS, Tuberculosis, and Malaria Act of 2003.

The newly enacted law, which would be known as the President's Emergency Plan for AIDS Relief (PEPFAR), was a turning point in U.S. foreign aid. President Bush gravely told the assembled crowd that they were witnessing an "historic moment, as our nation sets forth on a great mission of rescue. The United States of America has a long tradition of sacrifice in the cause of freedom. And we've got a long tradition of being generous in the service of humanity. We are the nation of the Marshall Plan, the Berlin Airlift, and the Peace Corps. And now we're the nation of the Emergency Plan for AIDS Relief."

He was not exaggerating. Over the next twenty years, PEPFAR would prove to be the most impactful global health initiative in human history, saving more than 26 million lives around the world and turning the tide in the fight against HIV. In 2024 alone, PEPFAR supported more than 20 million people on antiretroviral treatment, provided testing services for more than 83 million people, and prevented nearly 8 million babies from being born with HIV.

The legislation had just been passed by the Senate and sent to the president that morning. Bush did not want to waste any time signing it. In fact, he told the packed auditorium, "Every day of delay means 8,000 more AIDS deaths in Africa and 14,000 more infections—every day, 14,000 more people will be infected." He repeated the last statistic to make sure it sank in.

Too much time—too many lives—had been wasted already. Since the emergence of the HIV epidemic in 1981, three American presidents had either ignored or underestimated the growing global crisis, failing to mount a serious response. By 2003, between 20 and 25 million people had died, and the outlook was worsening. Globally, life expectancy was plummeting, construction of new orphanages could not keep pace with the ever-increasing number of parentless children, and public health experts were warning of the loss of an entire generation of working-age adults across Africa.

Among the heads of state gathered behind President Bush as he spoke was Dr. Kenneth Kaunda, the former president of Zambia. He had founded the Kenneth Kaunda Children of Africa Foundation, a national organization to support HIV orphans, after his own son died of HIV, orphaning Kaunda's grandchildren. Bush concluded his remarks to commemorate the enactment of PEPFAR: "The United States of America has the power and we have the moral duty to help. And I'm proud that our blessed and generous nation is fulfilling that duty." As the crowd applauded, Bush shook hands with Dr. Kaunda, knowing that the U.S. government had acted too slowly to save the Zambian leader's son, but hoping that it would not be too late for the next generation.

Earlier that same day, May 27, 2003, 7,600 miles to the southeast in Tanzania, a twenty-one-year-old with a scraggly beard and blistered feet was watching the sun rise from 18,000 feet above sea level. My heart was racing and my head was pounding, so I welcomed the brief respite to watch the sun creep over Mawenzi Peak, feeling those first rays punch through the pink and orange clouds to warm my icy nose and cheeks. But I did not have time to bask for long, and after a minute I forced myself to get back to the task I had set out on four days earlier: reaching the summit of Kilimanjaro, the highest point in Africa.

The sunrise was breathtaking—at least it took what little breath I had left. But it was also a reminder that I was moving too slowly. My trekking partner and I had left camp for our summit push just after midnight, under a canvas of pulsating stars so bright I thought I must be hallucinating. Now, six hours later, we should have nearly reached Uhuru Peak. But our guide had unexpectedly turned back hours earlier due to a bout of malaria and, in the confusion and darkness, we had decided to go on, led by a porter who spoke no English. My Swahili was serviceable, but even that did not help much, as the only words our new guide seemed to utter were the Kili mantra *pole pole* (go slowly), and he had recently even stopped saying that as the sky began to brighten. Now the dawn illuminated how much ground we still needed to cover, and confirmed what I had suspected for hours: We were moving too damn *pole pole*.

We still had over a thousand feet of elevation to gain. Soon the temperature would rise, and the melting snow and ice would loosen our path, making it impossible to continue upward. We were behind schedule, had lost our trusted guide, and if we were going to make it, we were going to have to disregard our new guide's only advice. Perhaps my aching head was an early symptom of severe altitude sickness and it was unsafe for me to continue. Maybe it was time to turn around.

But that was not going to happen. I wanted to reach the summit and, splitting headache and all, I was getting impatient. We needed to hurry. Screw *pole pole*, I had a new plan: We were not going to stop again until we reached the peak. One foot in front of the other, no matter what it took, we were going to make it. That was my pep talk, ostensibly for my trekking partner's benefit, but at least as much for my own. And then we were off again. The rest of the way was a slog—two steps forward, one slide back—but we did not give up.

Like the lawmakers in Washington, we got to celebrate that day, even though we, too, were late. Just after 9 a.m., we reached Uhuru Peak, elevation 19,340 feet. As I touched the sign that marked the summit of Kilimanjaro, I was overwhelmed by a sense of joy and accomplishment. I was surprised to realize there were tears in my eyes. Crying was extremely rare for me. In fact, I wouldn't cry again for another twenty-two years.

Happy as I was to have made it to the summit, I didn't dare linger for long, as the altitude sickness seemed to be worsening. My eyes were bulging and my head felt ready to explode at any moment. So I tried to catch my breath, snapped a few pictures, and started the long trek home. As the throbbing behind my eyes gradually subsided over the two-day descent, my mind wandered to what I was journeying back to.

Kilimanjaro was the culmination of a formative six months for me. One week earlier, I had taken a bus to Arusha, our base camp for the climb, following the completion of a college study-abroad program in Nairobi, Kenya. I had spent the 2003 spring semester in a program at the School for International Training called "Kenya: Development, Health, and Society."

Back home I was studying international development and foreign affairs at Tulane University, so I was familiar with much of the theory and history but, before deciding if this might be the right career path for me, I wanted to check out what it looked like in person. I was hooked right away. I fell in love with Kenya—the people, the food, the music, the culture. Nairobi was vibrant and frenetic and loud and ever-changing. There was too much traffic, too much pollution, too much crime, but there was a pervasive optimism that things were getting better, and everyone wanted to talk about it. Only a month before I arrived, the country had held the fairest and safest elections in its history, in which the reform candidate, Mwai Kibaki, pulled off an upset, winning the presidency over Uhuru Kenyatta, the outgoing president's handpicked successor. For the first time, young Kenyans felt that their government was accountable to them, and that they could openly criticize those in power without fear of retribution. The era of repression was in the rearview mirror, and there was nothing but the open road ahead.

But there was one thing—one terrible, dark cloud—that no one wanted to talk about. Amid all the progress and optimism, HIV was ravaging the country, affecting every city and town, every community, every family. The disease threatened Kenya's very future.

By 2003, the U.S. and other high-income countries had long since developed and implemented the tools to control the HIV epidemic within their health systems. Yet in Kenya, and throughout the developing world, it was wreaking havoc on a colossal scale. The life expectancy for the average Kenyan had fallen by 15 percent, to fifty-one years, the lowest level in decades. Such a drop was unprecedented in the time that humans have kept such records. The only comparable reductions were in isolated countries during the world's most destructive wars, and even in those cases the rates quickly bounced back after the conflicts ended.

In Kenya, the signs were not pointing to a quick rebound. Death was ubiquitous; attending funerals felt like a weekly routine. Among the country's adult population, 6.7 percent were HIV positive, and such a diagnosis was tantamount to a death sentence. I traveled to cities and rural areas, visiting health clinics, hospitals, orphanages, religious organizations, and community centers. Everywhere I went, I saw the same despair: the fear and grieving of families who did not have the resources to access lifesaving treatment, the loneliness of children who had lost their parents, the overwhelmed clinicians and health workers unable to provide comfort to so many patients, the determination of community leaders tirelessly working to provide consolation to their constituents and to collect donations for funeral costs from exhausted relatives and neighbors.

It was heartbreaking and extremely frustrating to witness; Kenya was on the brink of losing nearly an entire generation to HIV, a disease that was fully manageable in other parts of the world. Every day, I was faced with the same question: How could the rich countries of the world—my country—stand by and let so many people suffer when we had the technology and the resources to solve the problem?

Even then, I knew that USAID had a key role to play. The agency was already there. I saw USAID's iconic handshake logo emblazoned on buildings, vehicles, and equipment throughout Kenya. I saw USAID staff attending the occasional UN meetings we were allowed to observe. Whenever I saw the USAID logo, I felt pride in my country. That logo was a reminder that the U.S. cared about suffering in the world, and that we were committed to helping. By the end of my semester in Kenya, I had decided that I would work at USAID one day.

When I finally reached the bottom of Kilimanjaro, I stopped by an internet café in Arusha. I read an article about the enactment of PEPFAR. It felt as if the U.S. government was recognizing the urgency to act at the same time I was. My country had just reaffirmed its commitment to developing countries that they "will not fight alone" in the war against disease and poverty. I was ready to join the battle.

3.

A Lifelong Dream

I grew up in Lexington, Massachusetts, "the birthplace of American liberty," as the town is reverently referred to by its residents. Our home was less than a quarter mile from the site where the American Revolution began. A monument there immortalized the famous words uttered by Captain John Parker as the battle was about to commence: "Stand your ground. Do not fire unless fired upon, but if they mean to have a war, let it begin here."

As a kid, those words resonated with me. I realize that might sound strange if you grew up somewhere else, but indoctrination into the history of the American Revolution was a rite of passage for all young Lexingtonians. Each year on Patriots' Day (for the nonobservant, that's the third Monday in April), I would awaken at 5 a.m. to the sound of my father, adorned in his tricorn hat, shouting: "The British are coming! The British are coming!" Bleary-eyed, my brother and sister and I would bundle up—Massachusetts weather could be quite cold two hours before sunrise in mid-April—and walk to the Green to watch the annual reenactment of the Battle of Lexington.

From a young age, I tried to emulate Captain Parker's stubborn bravery. When I saw something that I felt was wrong in the world, I considered it my patriotic duty to do something about it, even if the odds were stacked against me. Following Parker's historic advice, I would stand my ground. Most of the time, however, this manifested in pointless power struggles with my parents or teachers, sometimes both. My "patriotism" in those days was heavier on the stubbornness, lighter on the bravery.

There was the time in fourth grade when a classmate lost her necklace during recess, but our tyrannical teacher refused to let her go out to the playground to find it. I started a chant that the rest of the class took up in unison: "Let her go! Let her go! Let her go!" Our teacher did not let her go, but he did call my parents to tell them that I had yet again disrupted class.

Then there was the time in ninth grade that I suspected that my social studies teacher was not reading our daily writing assignments and instead randomly assigning a grade of check, check plus, or check minus to each student on a whim. When I told my parents of the presumed injustice, and my plans to prove it, my exasperated mother pleaded with me to stand down. Nope. For the next two-page writing assignment, I wrote a word salad. No sentences, just random nonsense like "oranges loincloth temper spaghetti." Sure enough, when the teacher handed back my paper the next day, I received a check plus. Elated, I showed my mother the evidence when I got home that afternoon and told her my plan to expose the malfeasance. To my disappointment, Mom was not impressed. My mother, Peggy, a social worker, was studying for her doctorate in psychology, which she would complete the following year. But she did not need to be a licensed psychologist to know that my hotheadedness was going to get me into real trouble one day.

That same year, I joined the high school debate team in an effort to find a more constructive outlet for my argumentative tendencies. My brother, David, was a senior at the time, and the captain of the debate team. Three years older than me, David—who would grow up to be an investigative journalist—was always looking out for me. When I was in elementary school he heroically brandished a hockey stick to scare off a group of bullies who had been chasing me from the bus stop. He taught me everything he knew about debate, and I ran with it. By my senior year, I was nationally ranked, traveling the country to compete at the most prestigious debate tournaments.

That summer, I got my first taste of working in government as an intern for my representative in the Massachusetts House of Representatives. My father, Peter, a law professor at Northeastern University, had instilled the virtues of public service in me my whole life. At the time, he was serving as an elected official on the Lexington Board of Selectmen. He also worked for Michael Dukakis during his tenure as governor of Massachusetts and during his unsuccessful run for president in 1988. This was my chance to learn firsthand about the gears of government, and I was hooked from the start. I was excited to walk into the golden-domed Massachusetts State House each morning to watch the representatives engage with their constituents, propose legislation, and maneuver for votes.

But thanks to a brief moment of ineptitude, my career in government got off to an inauspicious start. One day in my second week on the job, I was tasked with bringing a bill to the Speaker's office to be submitted for a floor vote. I don't remember the content, just that it had been signed by several representatives and felt like the most important thing I had ever held in my possession. I stopped in the bathroom on my way through the State House's labyrinth hallways and, in a flash of horror I will never forget, I accidentally dropped the folder containing the bill directly into the toilet. In a panic, I fished it out and ran to the sink to dry it off. I spent what felt like hours holding each of a dozen pages under the blow-dryer, praying that no one would walk into the bathroom to witness how I had desecrated the democratic process. Luckily, no one came in, and I delivered the bill, only slightly worse for wear, to the waiting clerk.

During my freshman year at Tulane, my instinct to stand up against the improper use of authority got me in trouble once again, this time with me ending up in a jail cell. I attended my first Mardi Gras parade in February 2001, a raucous street party with marching bands, street performers, and scores of parade floats, each ridden by dozens of masked revelers tossing fistfuls of colorful bead necklaces toward the cheering onlookers. Amid the chaotic celebration, I noticed a friend of mine being roughly escorted, in handcuffs, by two police officers. Just before he was shoved into the back of a police cruiser, I asked my friend what had happened, and learned that he had taken a handful of beads from a passing float, rather than waiting for them to be thrown to him. I was shocked that he was being arrested for taking an item that was so casually being strewn throughout the streets.

(Following the last floats of the parade, cleanup crews sweep the streets of the thousands of unclaimed beads to prevent them from clogging the drains.)

I pleaded with the police officers to let my friend go. He had not known that taking the beads was a crime, I said, and certainly he had learned his lesson. The officers ignored me. I asked them to at least tell me where they were taking him so that I could arrange for his release once he was booked. Again, no response. When my friend tried to communicate something to me through the open passenger door, one of the officers barked at him to shut up. At that point, I asked the officers for their names and badge numbers, a subtle reminder that they were supposed to be public servants, protecting and serving the community. This got their attention, but unfortunately, not in the way I had hoped.

"You want my name and badge number?" one of the officers scoffed. "No problem, kid. It'll be on your arrest report. Hands behind your back."

As I sat next to my friend in the back of the cruiser, waiting to be taken to central lockup at Orleans Parish Prison, a high school band marched by performing an instrumental rendition of the Rolling Stones' "You Can't Always Get What You Want." To this day, that song reminds me of the ride to central lockup as I asked myself if I was ever going to learn to pick my battles.

Eventually, I did. The Mardi Gras parade incident certainly helped. And I found out a lot about myself during college, as I learned that there were too many problems in the world to tackle them all at once. But without question, the best thing I found at Tulane was Jordanna Berres-Paul, from Portland, Oregon. We met as freshmen, and developed a close friendship over the next three years, before I finally got up the nerve to ask her out. She was the unusual combination of high school valedictorian and captain of the cheerleading squad, which summed her up well: Jordanna was smart, talented, ambitious, fun, and beautiful.

From the moment we met, I knew she was one of a kind. In the first few weeks of college, at a time when I was still trying to impress potential friends by pretending to be into bands like Dispatch and Incubus, I hitched a ride with Jordanna and one of her friends to the grocery store. When the Knack's "My Sharona" came on the radio, Jordanna immediately turned it up, and then proceeded to shamelessly—and tunelessly—belt out every word at top volume. This future karaoke master was more comfortable in her own skin than anyone I've ever met, before or since. Jordanna taught me that true strength is having confidence in being who I am. Most important, she had no problem telling me when I was being an idiot, and with her help, I was able to mostly keep out of trouble.

We both studied abroad as juniors, me in Kenya, Jordanna in Spain, and after we returned to New Orleans we grew closer than ever our senior year. For the first time in my life, I had plans for the future, and I was hoping Jordanna would be a part of them. By graduation in 2004, I was pretty sure that Jordanna was the person I wanted to spend the rest of my life with, so when she found work in New York City that summer, I followed her there. We lived in Brooklyn, and were married in 2010, figuring we must be soulmates if we still loved each other after six years of living together in a shoebox-sized apartment.

After two years working for the New York State legislature, I went to Brooklyn Law School to study international human rights law, never wavering from my goal of one day working at USAID. When I graduated in 2010, I was accepted into the Presidential Management Fellows Program, the federal government's premier recruitment tool for future leaders seeking careers in public service. I served for two years at the U.S. Department of Housing and Urban Development before my dream position finally opened up at USAID. Moving to Washington with our six-week-old son, Zander, now in tow, I was giddy to start the career I had been working toward for almost ten years. I remember the excitement of walking into the Ronald Reagan Building on Pennsylvania Avenue for my first day on the tuberculosis team in USAID's Bureau for Global Health; I had finally made it.

The team was made up of an extremely impressive group of doctors, epidemiologists, and public health specialists, including some of the world's leading experts on tuberculosis control and prevention. I quickly got a firsthand look at their expertise. In 2018, following a trip to India that included several site visits, my routine TB skin test turned up positive. I had contracted the disease, joining an estimated 2 billion people worldwide carrying latent TB infection. Alarmed, I asked one of the doctors on my team what I should do. She recommended that I start treatment, but also told me not to worry: She also had contracted latent TB. (A person with latent TB infection carries the tuberculosis bacteria in their body, but has no symptoms and cannot spread the disease, as the bacteria are inactive, contained by a healthy immune system. In contrast, active TB disease occurs when the bacteria begin rapidly multiplying, usually triggered by a weakened immune system, causing symptoms and making the person contagious. Most TB infections remain latent; only approximately 10 percent of latent TB cases develop into active TB.) To drive this point home, she walked me around the office, polling the team members on whether they had been infected. Nearly half of them confirmed they had.

It was an honor to be working alongside such a dedicated and decorated team of experts, who were promoting research on new TB drugs and vaccines, and identifying promising innovations to support the sick and expand healthcare access to the remotest areas of the countries where we worked. This group was negotiating with host governments, civil society organizations, and UN agencies to raise the bar of national and international standards for diagnosing, treating, and preventing TB, just as other teams throughout USAID were doing the same to promote food security, economic opportunity, and human rights.

But USAID was not just a hub of technical expertise in global health and other development sectors. It was also a donor agency, responsible for managing contracts and distributing funds to other organizations that would do the work on-site. Most of my team had no experience—or interest—in federal procurement rules, and so it was my responsibility to transform the ideas of the technical tuberculosis experts into a cost-effective portfolio of contracts that would successfully accomplish their goals. It was a great job, and I was good at it, substantially improving the efficiency of our TB investments within a few years.

I worked on the TB team for eight years and then, after a brief hiatus in a different part of USAID, I became the Global Health Bureau's director of the Office of Policy, Programs, and Planning (a typical federal government alliterative mouthful that someone had years earlier shortened to "P3"). Simply put, my job was to ensure that USAID had the resources it needed to improve global health, and that we were using these resources efficiently to achieve as much positive impact as possible.

That was my position at USAID in November 2024. My discussion with Jordanna on that Tuesday evening on the week of Thanksgiving was a helpful reminder that my job sometimes meant implementing priorities that I didn't entirely agree with. As usual, her advice got me back on track. I spent Wednesday working with my team to concoct an ambitious timeline to move all the funding for the departing administration's global health priorities, in the event that Congress refused to lift its hold. While it was not the approach I would have taken, it would at least ensure that critical funding for the World Health Organization and for family planning programs could be used quickly. Even during a stressful week like that one, I loved my job and I couldn't imagine anything else I would rather do.

The next day, Jordanna and I bustled around the kitchen, preparing to host a small army for Thanksgiving dinner. In addition to our family of four, the guest list included my parents and my sister, who lived in D.C.; my brother and his family, who were visiting from New York; my mother-in-law, in town for the holiday from Oregon; and a few other relatives and friends. A pecan pie joined an apple torte and a smattering of other desserts on the counter, battling for space with the stuffing and potatoes that were waiting to go in the oven when the turkey and rolls came out. Cooking was a welcome distraction, and it was nice to take a breather from a tense week of work. The guests arrived and we all ate and drank and laughed and enjoyed spending time together. I think everyone made an effort to focus the conversation on anything but politics. But, inevitably, the topic of the presidential transition eventually came up and everyone shared their predictions of when exactly I would lose my job.

"Your rolls are pretty tasty, Nicholas," joked my younger sister, Liza. "Worst-case scenario, maybe you open a bakery?" Liza had spent her childhood in the unenviable position of, year after year, being placed in classes with teachers whom I had driven nuts three years prior and were wary of seeing another Enrich on their roster. Against all odds, she had won them over time and time again, and now she was a high school chemistry teacher herself. She had earned the right to tease me, even at as tense a time as this.

My mother did not see the humor. "Seriously, what *would* you want to do if you lose your job?" she prodded.

I answered honestly: "I have absolutely no idea."

4.

Guessing Game

"You need to listen to yesterday's Joe Rogan show," I said to my team on Wednesday, December 4. There was an audible groan in the conference room. I am not a regular listener. In fact, I don't think I had ever sat through an episode of *The Joe Rogan Experience* before. But this one was a must-listen.

Every change in administration brings with it a new set of opportunities and challenges for the career civil service. As we awaited the arrival of President-elect Trump's team, we tried to learn everything we could about the new president's plans for USAID. We wanted to be as prepared as possible for the coming changes in policy and approach so we would be able to advise the new administration on how best to implement them.

First on the assigned reading list was *Project 2025*, the policy agenda prepared by the Heritage Foundation that was likely to serve as a blueprint for the Trump administration's priorities. *Project 2025* had become a political hot potato during the campaign, with Democrats claiming that the radical cuts to the federal bureaucracy outlined in its pages were a harbinger of suffering for American families under a Trump presidency. Trump publicly distanced himself from the document, claiming he did not even know what was in it. But now that he had won the election, we read the portion on USAID carefully, bracing for the worst.

We were relieved to see that *Project 2025* did not call for the elimination of USAID. In a twenty-eight-page section on foreign aid, the authors recognized the critical value of the agency:

> USAID helps communities to lead their own development journeys by reducing the impact of conflict; preventing hunger and the spread of pandemic disease; and counteracting the drivers of violence, instability, transnational crime, and other threats. In alignment with U.S. national security interests, the agency promotes American prosperity through initiatives that expand markets for U.S. exports; encourage innovation; create a level playing field for U.S. businesses; and support more stable, resilient, and democratic societies that are less likely to act against American interests and more likely to respect family, life, and religious liberty.

Still, *Project 2025*'s assessment was by no means entirely positive. There was aggressive criticism of the direction USAID had taken over the past four years, some of it valid and some of it outlandish. For example: "The Biden Administration has deformed the agency by treating it as a global platform to pursue overseas a divisive political and cultural agenda that promotes abortion, climate extremism, gender radicalism, and interventions against perceived systemic racism. It has dispensed with decades of bipartisan consensus on foreign aid and pursued policies that contravene basic American values and have antagonized our partners in Asia, Africa, and Latin America." This assertion was unfair and bore no relation to the reality of our work. But it was nonetheless worrisome because it suggested there was a wide chasm we would need to bridge to demonstrate the value of our work to the incoming administration.

But even more concerning than its disparaging of the agency's current political leadership were the cryptic accusations against the career staff during Trump's first term. Without any supporting context or evidence, the document proclaimed as fact that "the Trump Administration agenda for USAID was undercut from the outset . . . by recalcitrant career personnel."

Having worked at USAID throughout the first Trump administration, I knew this statement to be false.

I had personally implemented the agenda of Administrator Mark Green during Trump's first term and, together with my colleagues, had vigorously carried out his policy framework, the Journey to Self-Reliance. Even though I felt that parts of the agenda were problematic, I recognized that my role was to implement the policies of the president and his administration, and I ensured that those policies were executed coherently and lawfully.

For example, the Trump administration instituted a policy called Protecting Life in Global Health Assistance, which barred contractors that supported abortion services with their private funds from receiving any U.S. global health funding—even though those contractors were already legally prohibited from using federal funds to support or promote abortion. The new policy was similar to the so-called Mexico City Policy that had been instituted by every Republican administration since Ronald Reagan, but expanded to bar access to all global health funds, whereas previous versions had only barred access to family planning funds. I was concerned that PLGHA was overly broad, cutting off resources to partners implementing critical activities that were unrelated to abortion or family planning in any way, putting those programs at risk of failure. However, it was the administration's policy, and I faithfully implemented it. I served as the PLGHA focal point for the TB division to ensure that the policy was enforced across all our contracts.

It was extremely frustrating to read in *Project 2025* that the USAID workforce was being portrayed as recalcitrant and undercutting. But there was no point dwelling on the negative. My colleagues and I would learn to work with the new administration, and in the meantime, once we got past the partisan bluster, *Project 2025* appeared to be full of opportunities to improve our agency. After reading the document, I instructed my division chiefs to connect the specific recommendations in *Project 2025* to those changes that we were currently pursuing to increase efficiency at USAID. Ramona Godbole, my deputy, shared my optimism. "If these are their priorities for USAID, we'll be able to push through a lot of the efficiencies we've been working on—procurement reform, localization, earlier access to funding, private sector engagement—it's all in there," she said. She was already starting to compute the ways we could use the document to improve the way we worked.

We also participated in Washington's quadrennial game of guessing who was likely to be picked as political appointees for our agency. On a near-daily basis, a new name would make its way through the rumor mill as a possible USAID administrator—everyone from Ted Cruz to Ivanka Trump. I read and listened to everything I could find about all of them, searching for anything that might hint at their priorities for global health.

As Inauguration Day approached, while many questions remained, I thought I had a pretty good idea of what the changes at USAID might look like. The new Trump team would likely switch course on investing in climate resilience and family planning, banning new funds to the WHO and organizations that used other funds to support abortion services. (I say "other funds" because, contrary to the lies of certain interest groups, no USAID funds are used to support abortion services. Providing or promoting abortions using U.S. foreign assistance funds is prohibited by law, and the agency was very careful to ensure that this prohibition was strictly enforced.) The Trump administration was more likely to focus on leveraging the private sector and faith-based organizations, aiming to fast-track self-sufficiency in the countries where we worked, with the goal of reducing our foreign aid footprint over time. My job, as it had been from 2017 to 2021, would be to help them get there.

All of that felt manageable. But the Rogan podcast was different; there was no way to put a positive spin on it. On the evening of December 3, my old high school friend Steve recommended it in our group text thread. A Trump supporter with seemingly unlimited bandwidth for podcast consumption, Steve had somehow digested Rogan's full two-hour-and-forty-five-minute show immediately upon its release earlier that day, and he was excited for me to hear it. "Lots of discussion of USAID, so I'm now nearly convinced that Nick is full-on deep state (I kid, I kid)," he texted. I was unfamiliar with Joe Rogan's guest, Mike Benz, but I had a sense of the scale of Rogan's audience, and my friend was immersed in conservative social media trends. So I started the episode the next day on my morning run, intrigued, if a bit skeptical, as part of my research into the policy priorities that President-elect Trump might have in store.

Mike Benz, a political appointee at the State Department in the first Trump administration and an influential crusader against the "censorship industrial complex," was clearly not a fan of USAID. I wrote off his initial portrayal of my beloved agency as unhinged paranoia:

> USAID is very notorious. It's sort of a switch player. There's no aid in USAID. By the way, your brain is being tricked when you see the phrase USAID. It's not an aid organization. The "AID" in USAID stands for U.S. Agency for International Development. It is developing internationally around the world. . . . USAID is effectively a switch player to assist the Pentagon on the national security front, to assist the State Department on the national interest front, or to assist the intelligence community on a sort of clandestine operations front.

As the interview went on, I began to see how Benz's unsubstantiated and disjointed arguments might find a welcome audience in the incoming administration. His claim was that USAID was not really a development agency at all, but a manipulative tool of the "deep state" to spread a system of international censorship designed to perpetuate its own power, at the expense of free speech and democracy. From this premise he extrapolated that USAID's campaign to support countries to combat misinformation, primarily in the name of promoting democratic institutions, was a direct threat to the interests of Elon Musk, specifically to his ubiquitous social media company, X. Speaking ill of misinformation, he argued, would lead to regulation and even the banishment of X and similar platforms around the world, eroding free speech and silencing the voices of those who challenged the power of the entrenched elite.

This was the first time I had heard USAID painted in "enemy of the people" brushstrokes from within Trump's circle, and I did not like it.

Benz's thesis was extremely short on evidence and rife with logical fallacy, but it was a convenient theory for those looking to make major changes at USAID, and it was not hard to imagine that Trump or some of his powerful friends might have been listening. Infuriating as it was to hear Benz slander USAID, I wanted my team to be aware of his perspective.

My team was as shocked as I was. Alyssa Jernigan, GH's budget director, reacted with comic disbelief, joking that Benz had given USAID far more credit for sophisticated, devious subversion than we deserved. I had hired Alyssa the previous year to modernize our budget formulation process, and she did not disappoint. In her first fiscal year on the job, she had fully revamped how we prepared our budget, making it more strategic and inclusive while reducing timelines and eliminating unneeded bottlenecks—all while she planned her wedding for October 1, the day after the fiscal year ended. Armed with an infectious sense of humor, she would occasionally roll her eyes at me during our check-in meetings when I couldn't keep up with her. She was a rising star in GH, and I fully expected to work for Alyssa one day, likely, I surmised, as the future administrator of USAID.

"He's basically accusing us of going rogue and overthrowing governments whenever we feel like it," Alyssa said. "Clearly he had no clue how we actually work here. We are too afraid to reprogram a hundred dollars without getting permission from six different bureaus at State." Then, an instant later, her smile dropped and she half whispered: "You don't think he'll be appointed as administrator, do you?" We both laughed nervously.

Our fears were realized a couple days later, when it became clear that Elon Musk had listened to Rogan's December 3 podcast. There was no reason to believe that USAID had even registered on Musk's radar before this. He had never mentioned the agency on X. But once he heard Rogan's interview with Benz, the agency apparently became his public enemy number one. On December 10, Musk made his first-ever reference to USAID, retweeting another user's summary of the podcast: "Mike Benz just revealed everything. On *The JRE* [*Joe Rogan Experience*], he exposed why USAID is a tool for control, not aid." From that point on, Musk became obsessed with the agency, amplifying Benz's anti-USAID message to his more than 200 million followers. He would retweet or mention Benz in dozens of posts trashing USAID over the next two months.

Despite Musk's newfound interest, I dismissed Benz's musings as little more than fodder for spy novel conspiracy theories.

5.

Ominous Signs

By this point, several weeks had passed since the election, with no sign of a landing team from the incoming Trump administration. Everything we had heard, however, was that the second Trump transition would not be like the first. So we continued to wait for them to show up.

We were in good hands. The transition team for GH was led by my boss, Julie Wallace, the bureau's lead deputy assistant administrator. A former Peace Corps volunteer and a nurse by training, Julie had worked at USAID for more than twenty years, and over that time had risen to the top civil service position in global health. Brilliant, savvy, and working seemingly twenty-four hours a day, Julie set high standards for the bureau and then led by example to make sure they were met. Nothing happened in GH that Julie did not know about. Through her green-rimmed glasses, her sharp eyes seemed not to miss anything, ever; there was no rule, process, or memo that Julie was not familiar with. No one was more experienced or qualified than Julie to represent global health to the incoming administration.

Finally, in mid-December, Trump's landing team arrived, led by Cartwright Weiland, a State Department alumnus of the first Trump administration. The landing team's initial briefings focused on agency-wide operations, management, and human resources. In GH, we eagerly awaited our chance to showcase our work, confident that Weiland and his team would be impressed by the expertise and experience of our staff and the results we were achieving—lives saved, access to healthcare expanded, enhanced early warning systems for outbreaks, infectious diseases controlled and in some cases eliminated.

But our turn never came. Weiland's crew showed no interest in global health or, for that matter, in international development at all. They had questions, but they were not about foreign aid. Instead, they were laser-focused on staff. How many people worked on gender equality, how many on DEI, how many on climate change, how many on policy? Which staff were contractors, which were federal employees? How many staffers were tenured, how many were still in their probationary period? How many staff worked in-person, how many were remote? How many days a week were people in the office?

Each bureau was tasked with compiling answers to these questions. But some were difficult to answer. Does everyone in the Office of Population and Reproductive Health work, by definition, on gender equality? How about in the Office of Maternal and Child Health and Nutrition? What does it mean to work on "policy"? As human resources teams across the agency set about sorting staff into various categories, fear and speculation began to spread.

Natalia Machuca, the deputy director for GH's Office of Professional Development and Management Support—bureaucratic jargon that could just as easily be reduced to simply "HR"—was responsible for verifying the requested staffing information with each office within the GH Bureau. A trained microbiologist, Natalia had worked in global health at USAID for fifteen years and was one of the most respected people in the bureau. Only recently had she switched over from working on GH programs—most recently in malaria—to take on a formal human resources role, but she had been strengthening our staffing capacity on an informal basis for over a decade. More of the bureau's eight hundred employees called Natalia their mentor than anyone else. A few years ago I was on a hiring panel with Natalia and accidentally joined an interview five minutes before it was scheduled to start. To my surprise, Natalia was already there. When I asked her why she was early, she told me cheerfully that she always joins interviews early, so she can put a nervous interviewee at ease before the full panel joins and the formal discussion begins.

But despite all the goodwill Natalia had built up during her career in GH, no one wanted to talk to her about her current assignment. Everyone knew that Natalia would do all she could to protect the staff, but many were concerned that the Trump administration would use the information she had been ordered to collect to institute mass firings. Presumably they couldn't fire everyone, so who was safe and who was at risk? Would they start with the contractors, who lacked civil service protections? Would they go after the staff who worked on policy, the administration's opening blow in its quest to dismantle the "deep state"? Would remote workers be terminated if they didn't immediately move to Washington, even if that meant pulling their children out of school midyear?

One morning in late December, Alyssa came into my office, looking miserable. She possessed an uncanny ability to compartmentalize her fears and concerns in order to focus on the work, so as soon as I saw the worry in her eyes, I knew we had a problem. Her team was responsible for pushing through funds for the remaining Biden administration priorities, and she was having trouble keeping everyone focused amid the swirling rumors.

"They're coming to me in tears," she said, "and I don't know what to tell them. They're afraid that if their names are on memos to move funds for reproductive health or WHO, they're going to be fired as soon as the new administration comes in. I'm trying not to speculate about what's coming, but I can't in good conscience tell them that won't happen for sure."

She didn't say it, but I recognized that there was risk for her as well—and for me. I told her that we would keep all her team member's names off the funding memos and mine would be the only name listed. It was highly unlikely, I reasoned, that I would lose my job for moving funds under the direction of the agency's leadership. And if that *was* how they were going to play it, I was almost certainly going to be in deep trouble anyway, regardless of these funding actions.

There was good reason for the staff to be alarmed. The ominous inquiries the landing team was pursuing were a stark reminder of Russell

Vought's threatening remarks during the campaign about federal employees. It was all too easy to make the link between Vought's plan to traumatize the federal workforce and the questions the landing team was now asking.

Still, I convinced myself that we were safe. Sure, our days of teleworking twice a week were probably numbered, and it might be a few years before we would again receive a normal annual pay raise. But we were career federal employees, protected by long-standing regulations established to ensure a nonpartisan and merit-based civil service. More important, we were the experts who administered congressionally enacted programs that saved lives and protected national security. What were they going to do? Fire us all? Have security kick us out of the building? Accuse us of being criminals?

Besides, even though we did not yet know who would be picked as our next administrator, we did know the nominee for secretary of state, Senator Marco Rubio, and he was a stalwart supporter of USAID. I couldn't imagine Trump making a better choice for the State Department in terms of protecting foreign aid. During his time in the Senate, Rubio had repeatedly sung the praises of USAID and the benefits of foreign assistance. For example, in 2015 he said:

> "A lot of times people say, 'Well, cut foreign aid.' Foreign aid is less than one percent of our budget. But foreign aid can make a difference when properly used. And if you ever have a chance, travel to the African continent and you will meet people who are alive today because of the American taxpayer-funded antiviral HIV medications that kept them alive. It will not be easy to radicalize people who are alive because the American taxpayer saved their lives and the lives of their children."

As recently as 2022, during the Biden administration, Rubio had advocated for prioritizing funding for USAID as a key tool to "counter the Chinese Communist Party's expanding global influence."

There was another oddity that made the nearing transfer of power different from the previous presidential transitions I had experienced: the

Department of Government Efficiency, which was to be overseen by Elon Musk. At first DOGE seemed no more threatening than a trolling internet joke that went a bit too far. Musk took the acronym from an internet dog meme, the same dog meme he had used years earlier to launch a joke cryptocurrency called Dogecoin, which spectacularly collapsed. The concept behind DOGE was, actually, laudable: bringing in an outsider to take a fresh look at federal agencies and programs to identify ways to reduce waste and increase efficiency. I'll admit that it was somewhat unnerving to hear Trump and Musk and their allies trumpeting DOGE as a tool to slash the federal bureaucracy, but I was not overly worried.

After all, the plan was light on details. It was not even clear whether or how DOGE would, or could, become a part of the government. And Musk's target of $2 trillion in savings was a figure so astronomical that I assumed this was more of an aspirational project than a real one. And if that really was the goal, USAID's paltry budget was too small to matter.

Naively, I was still looking for silver linings. As it became clear that DOGE really was coming, in one form or another, I went about preparing a list of opportunities to increase efficiency in global health programming at USAID. As the director of P3, this was already my job. And while USAID has always been one of the most cost-effective federal agencies in terms of return on investment, there was always room for improvement. I had several ideas, many of which I was already working on, and I was confident that DOGE would be thrilled to learn that we were ready to hand them a road map for some quick wins.

So I started to write up the plans. I wanted to change the way we structured our contracts to expand and strengthen our partnerships with local organizations. I had ideas to make USAID's investments contingent on a host government's commitment to increasing its financial contributions, thereby reducing its future need for U.S. aid. To increase the accountability of our largest international partners, I planned to design new incentives to ensure that payments were more directly tied to results. If DOGE ever came to ask me how to improve government efficiency at USAID, I was ready to tell them.

At the same time that we were preparing for the arrival of the incoming Trump administration, we were also working in overdrive to enact and institutionalize as many of the Biden administration's remaining priorities as possible in the final weeks of his term. This always happens with outgoing administrations, but especially when the incoming president represents the other political party, and even more so when the outgoing president has only served a single term.

Our normal timelines for making contracts, updating rules, and moving funds went out the window. We scrambled to expedite *everything*. We worked nights and weekends; we worked through Christmas and New Year's. We continued at that pace up to the final day of the term when the last political appointees turned in their badges and tendered their resignations. And we accomplished a ton. In the eighty-two days between Election Day and Inauguration Day, we enacted a new sector-wide global health development policy, we fully overhauled our rules for how USAID global health funds can be used, and we delivered more than $500 million to fight infectious diseases, expand access to primary healthcare, and provide family planning and reproductive health services around the world.

With all this going on, I did not have much time or energy left to speculate on the future of the agency or job security for myself and my colleagues. Like so much swirling smoke, there was no solid truth to the countless rumors that could be trusted. As difficult as it was, I tried to instead focus on what I could do to set our programs on the path to future success.

The mindset of productivity over dread started at the top. In early January, at a small, celebratory gathering at Atul Gawande's apartment in Washington's Mount Pleasant neighborhood, Atul announced that Julie Wallace would be in charge of GH following his mandatory resignation on January 20, until Trump appointed a new assistant administrator. He challenged her to be an inclusive and compassionate leader, to promote an environment where every staff member feels empowered to contribute their unique strengths toward achieving the shared goals of global health.

"Julie, you are the brain of the Global Health Bureau," Atul said. "You have all the expertise and knowledge of GH at your disposal. Now you will have the power. My only question is: How will you use it?"

While it was no surprise that Julie would be our interim leader, it was a relief to hear the announcement. With the gravity of Atul's question ("How will you use it?") echoing in my head, I couldn't fathom how I would have responded to such a challenge. I was grateful to not be in her shoes.

For her part, Julie was ready to lead. She presented a fearless front to the bureau, projecting strength and certainty at a time when so many felt powerless and confused. She tried to squelch the rumors of our demise and dissuaded supervisors from participating in worrisome and fruitless speculation. Instead she urged us all to concentrate on the task at hand. Her mantra, which she repeated many times each day, was "We're here to serve, it's as simple as that."

I soon learned that this was a facade. Even Julie was worried. After a team meeting where Atul reminded her to make sure to be welcoming to the incoming political appointees, I met alone with Julie.

"*Welcome* them?" she said. "I'm hearing that all senior staff might be fired on day one. I don't know how welcoming I can be if these are the kind of people we're dealing with."

She paused and took a deep breath, and the consternation on her face was replaced with a smile. Her split second of vulnerability was over. "Well, I guess, I'm here to serve . . . until I'm not," she said, and then got up to head to her next meeting.

This shook me. I knew that Julie was engaging regularly with the highest-ranking officials in the agency. If *she* was concerned about being fired, maybe I should be a bit more worried. But I tried to brush it off, reminding myself that there was no way she could know what was coming. Like the rest of us, Julie was only human after all, and I rationalized that she had just momentarily let her fear get the better of her.

On a late afternoon the week before Inauguration Day, we all crammed into an overcrowded conference room to bid a final farewell to Atul. One after another, career staff members thanked him for all his contributions to global health. On the videoconference screen, health officers at missions overseas chimed in, describing the progress achieved under his leadership. A colleague from Indonesia had woken up early to personally thank Atul for his visit with community health workers in his country, bringing hope of improved access to primary healthcare services to underserved areas. Another colleague from Malawi—with tears in her eyes—reminisced about how far the health programs in her country had come during Atul's term, emerging from the depths of COVID to now, just a couple years later, having established surveillance and early warning systems to prevent the next pandemic.

Finally, Julie presented Atul with a surprise gift: She had arranged to have a conference room named in his honor, forever enshrining his legacy at USAID. Atul offered his humble thanks, and then made an offhanded quip about how quickly the next administration might have the conference room restored to its previous name, "07.08.0E."

The allusion to Atul's impermanence was a bit of a downer. Hoping to revive the celebratory spirit, Julie faux-scolded him: "Atul, you should know by now: Never underestimate the power of the civil service!" Everyone laughed.

6.

Frozen (Days 1–7)

Finally, it was Inauguration Day. On Monday, January 20, 2025, Donald Trump was sworn in for a second term as president, this time inside the Capitol Rotunda, due to an unusually cold and blustery forecast.

At USAID, my colleagues and I were already exhausted from our grueling sprint to the finish line of the Biden administration. I, for one, really needed a break. While the timing was not perfect for a vacation, I convinced myself that it was okay; the new administration would be getting its bearings, and I'd be back before any major changes happened. And besides, we had a strong plan in place. Julie Wallace was in charge of global health until a new political appointee took over, ensuring stability during the transition. Julie reassured me that I should take a vacation, so that I would return recharged and ready for whatever came next. So off I went to British Columbia for a ski trip I had been planning for nearly two years.

I arrived in the Canadian Rockies that night, joining my podcast-obsessed friend, Steve, at the airport for the drive into the mountains. Arriving at our shabby rental condo, withered from the long travel day, Steve and I agreed to take quick showers and meet in thirty minutes to grab a bite to eat. I unpacked my bag and turned on the shower. As I waited for the water to heat up, I connected my phone to the rental's Wi-Fi. Ten minutes later, the steam creeping out from the crack below the bathroom door, I had forgotten all about the shower. I'd made the mistake of reading the news.

President Trump had signed twenty-six executive orders on his first day in office. EO 14169 was titled "Reevaluating and Realigning United States Foreign Aid." It directed federal agencies, for ninety days, to "immediately pause" the distribution of foreign aid to countries, NGOs, and others "pending reviews of such programs for programmatic efficiency and consistency with United States foreign policy."

This was not good. Skimming the executive order from my phone, my heart started to race. How could we do this without completely destabilizing our global health programs and immediately endangering people's lives? The order didn't affect a mere portion of our work; it stopped everything USAID did. The agency's primary function was to disburse development assistance funds. Rather than directly implementing projects itself, USAID provided funding through contracts to partner organizations—NGOs, contractors, foreign government entities, etc.—to carry out our programs on the ground. USAID set priorities, engaged with host governments, oversaw performance, and ensured accountability through rigorous monitoring and evaluation, but it was our contractors who implemented the programs. Without being able to move funds, our work would come to a screeching halt.

Ninety days might seem like a brief pause, but it was practically a lifetime for fragile supply chains—and it was literally a lifetime for newborn babies requiring emergency care or for children dying of acute malnutrition. I read the order again, more carefully this time, looking for clues about its scope and intent. Clearly, new contracts were prohibited, but what about our ongoing programs that had already received funds to operate? Could they continue their work? Wouldn't such a sweeping change include exceptions to protect human life or to protect American property?

I did not see any exceptions, but there was a vague reference to waivers for "specific programs." My colleagues and I would need to get started right away on figuring out how to advocate for a waiver for global health programs. And what about the foreign assistance reviews mentioned in the order? Maybe we could fast-track them for global health—we had, after all, already prepared detailed briefings on our programs, which explained their critical importance—and get the official green light to restart the programs before there were many problems.

My initial impression was that the wording of the executive order must have been a mistake. The goal of taking a fresh look at our programs before putting more money into them was reasonable. I had no doubts that our programs were justifiable, and if the new administration had ideas for how to improve them, I was eager to hear them. I understood the rationale for wanting to pause the issuance of new contracts as well. Most of our contracts were for five years, and it made sense that the new administration would want time to sign off on any new projects that were to start on their watch. But the order appeared to go far beyond that. It imposed a complete pause on all our work, including programs already active on the ground, which would have catastrophic results around the world—cutting patients off from treatment for deadly diseases, preventing distribution of food aid to starving children. That couldn't have been the intention. Could it?

My next thought was that, even though I had just arrived in British Columbia, I probably needed to get back to Washington right away. This was a mess that would require a major cleanup effort, and that was my job. Or maybe I was being too hasty. I still had no idea how the new administration would propose to implement the order. Like most executive orders, this one was quite broad, and would need to be supplemented by agency-specific guidance on how it would be instituted. Perhaps supplemental guidance would be issued in the next few days, and that would put my concerns to rest. If not, I could head home then to help find solutions to minimize disruptions to our programs.

A loud knock at my door startled me back to reality.

"C'mon, Nick," Steve said impatiently. "Let's go. I'm starving!" Wincing at his choice of words, I grabbed my coat and we headed out for dinner.

Back in Washington, career officials at USAID were also struggling to interpret the executive order. The agency's front office offered no guidance.

Although new political appointees had arrived on Inauguration Day, they offered no clarity, failing to send even an introductory note to their new workforce, to reach out to leaders from the various bureaus, or to engage in any of the other regular formalities that might be expected from an incoming leadership team hoping to make a first impression on their agency.

Their first word came on Tuesday, January 21, in the form of a curt, agency-wide notice from Ken Jackson, USAID's new acting deputy administrator, announcing that Jason Gray, a kindly and knowledgeable career official who had served as USAID's chief information officer for the previous two years, had been designated as the agency's acting administrator. Jason was an unexpected choice for the agency's top position, bypassing many career staff with far more technical expertise and experience. Between the surprise selection of Jason and the pleasantry-less email, the announcement increased the uncertainty surrounding who was actually in charge of USAID.

Without any guidance from the new political appointees, the agency's senior career leaders met to determine how to proceed with implementing the executive order. Career officials from each bureau teased out the implications for their programs based on different interpretations of the directive. The attendees were evenly divided into two groups. The first proposed that the executive order should be interpreted broadly, and all funding—new funds and funds already provided to contractors—should be frozen. This group argued that the directive clearly intended to pause all our programs, and to stop short of a full freeze would be to fail to implement the intent of the order. The second group argued that the order should be interpreted to only affect new funding, at least until supplemental guidance was issued. The language was too vague to apply the freeze to ongoing work, and there were potentially serious legal implications—not to mention programmatic implications—of cutting off contractor access to funds that had already been approved. It would be legally risky to implement such a sweeping order without clear political cover.

The first group retorted that the new administration was already wary of the civil service, and this was an opportunity to show them that we were serious about executing their policies. Even if there were unanswered questions about the executive order, they reasoned, the new administration had issued its first directive—a total pause on foreign aid—and the agency should comply in good faith. If we didn't, we risked being sidelined as the "deep state." By the meeting's end, the fear of being perceived as obstructionist won out over the legal concerns about complying. The career leadership agreed to preemptively institute a total freeze on all new contracts, as well as on any funding that might have already been issued under existing contracts.

Later that week, Secretary Rubio finally issued the anticipated supplemental guidance on the executive order. He directed USAID to "immediately issue stop-work orders" to contractors "until such time as the Secretary shall determine, following a review." Rubio's guidance confirmed my worst fears: The executive order was not just a pause on future funding or new projects, it was a complete halt on all our work.

Following Rubio's guidance, Jami Rodgers, USAID's senior procurement officer, immediately set to work drafting stop-work orders to be sent out to our contractors. Jami had worked in federal contracting for more than two decades with four federal agencies, and had come to USAID from NASA in 2023. Since his arrival, Jami had worked wonders, updating the agency's clunky and sluggish procurement systems and paving the way for new types of contracts that improved USAID's ability to hold contractors accountable for results. Nothing in his extensive contracting pedigree, however, had prepared him for the order he now received from the secretary of state to issue a blanket freeze to the thousands of active contracts of an entire agency. But he was determined to comply. Despite the outcry of contractual and legal questions, and objections and concerns from contracting officers stationed around the world, Jami pushed his team to execute the stop-work orders immediately.

As soon as the stop-work orders were delivered to USAID partners, directing them to cease their ongoing activities, questions began to pour back in. For an action that had never before been implemented on a mass scale, the directive to contractors to stop their work was woefully short on details. It provided no guidance on when they might receive payment for the work they had already completed, or whether they were permitted to spend funds to secure property, pay their staff, or protect the health or lives of the beneficiaries they were in the process of serving. What should they do with medicine that was already on ships en route to ports around the world? What about food that was sitting in warehouses in need of distribution? There were hundreds of millions of dollars' worth of perishable commodities that would expire and go to waste if contractors were not authorized to resume their work, commodities that the recipient governments were relying on to avoid shortages in their health systems.

Promises had been made, not just to governments, but also to people. Patients had been advised to return to clinics to receive test results. Now, without warning, those clinics would be closed, leaving patients undiagnosed and untreated. Within days, the health team at USAID in South Africa alerted the TB division in Washington that several clinical trials had been interrupted, preventing hundreds of tuberculosis patients who had recently been enrolled on novel treatment regimens from accessing their drugs. Without the medicine provided by USAID through the trials, there were no alternative options for the enrollees to receive treatment for the life-threatening infectious disease. The stop-work orders were in direct conflict with the ethical standards of an ongoing clinical trial, jeopardizing the reputations of renowned research institutions, not to mention the lives of the enrolled individuals, many of whom were children. Similar problems were reported in Vietnam, Zambia, and the Philippines. A ninety-day pause—even a fraction of that—was simply not feasible for dozens of clinical trials underway around the world.

Many contractors were entirely dependent on the reliable flow of USAID funds to continue their most basic operations and payroll. Even the largest international NGOs would be hard-pressed to remain in limbo for three months. With thousands of staff across dozens of countries— many of which had labor laws requiring months of advance notice prior to any layoffs—these contractors were forced into the untenable position of choosing between facing bankruptcy if they tried to maintain their payroll without receiving USAID funds or illegally furloughing their staff. Overnight, the stop-work orders had severely shaken the financial stability of many of USAID's partners.

Aside from money, what these governments and NGOs needed most were answers. Instead, their questions were met with silence. Unbeknownst to the contractors, USAID's new political leadership had issued a blanket ban on any external communications, which barred the agency's staff from responding to any inquiries. "Failure to abide by this directive, or any of the directives sent out earlier this week and in the coming weeks, will result in disciplinary action," Ken Jackson, the acting deputy administrator, warned in a memo sent to the entire agency.

The project managers at GH, who were accustomed to daily correspondence with their contractors, pleaded for guidance from Julie Wallace. Did Ken's message really mean that they couldn't send an email or make a phone call? Correct, she told them. As painful as it was, they could not attend external meetings or respond to external emails, even to let contractors know that they were banned from communicating with them.

Barred from engaging with the outside world, the agency failed to respond to the deluge of questions. USAID project managers were forced to ghost their contractors, unable to join regular meetings, or even to cancel the meetings they knew they would be unable to join. Instead, they were left to helplessly scroll through increasingly desperate email requests and listen to distraught voicemails asking how they could continue to operate their businesses.

In Canada later that day, feeling disconnected and very far away, I was wondering how my team was dealing with the rising pressure fueled by the combination of the executive order and the communications ban when I received a call from Ramona Godbole.

My deputy had had a bad day. Her voice quavered. I thought she might start to cry before she could tell me what was happening, but she forged ahead. "They started firing people today," she said.

She explained that Jason Gray had issued guidance on another of Trump's executive orders, "Ending Radical and Wasteful Government DEI Programs and Preferencing." The directive ordered the firing of staff working on issues of diversity, equity, inclusion, or accessibility. Further, it required all employees, under threat of disciplinary action, to report any activities or staff who appeared to be trying to subvert the intent of the executive order to DEIAtruth@opm.gov, an email address that evoked George Orwell's novel *Nineteen Eighty-Four*. Julie had no choice but to identify the five global health staff who focused on DEI, and they had been immediately terminated.

My heart sank. Two of the five had worked in my office and had served long careers advancing public health in a variety of roles. It was the administration's prerogative to end DEI programs, and our job to fully comply (even if the prescribed procedure to do so felt like a witch hunt). I had suspected that these individuals' job responsibilities would need to be revised so they could continue to help with our mission, while no longer focusing on DEI. But I couldn't believe they had been fired, just like that, simply for doing their jobs.

"I'm so sorry, Ramona," I said. I felt terrible that I hadn't been there, if only just to help say goodbye to my colleagues who had been so unfairly dismissed. I told her that I regretted having left town at such a terrible time. It was time for me to come home.

She disagreed and told me to stay. "There's no reason to come back. We're not doing anything here anyway. Everyone is miserable, we're just sitting around waiting for Julie to tell us there is something we can do."

I called Jordanna, told her what had happened, and said that I was torn over what to do next. "Do you really think you could do anything differently if you were there?" she asked. I knew I couldn't. Julie had things in as much control as she could, and there wasn't much I—or anyone—could do to help. But it felt as if I were abandoning my team during an emergency, and that I should be there, if only for the sake of solidarity.

Jordanna wasn't convinced: "So you're going to race home just to sit with your colleagues and be miserable together? Don't be a martyr, Nick.

If there was something you could do to help, that would be one thing, but don't pretend you're more important than you really are. I would just try to enjoy the trip. And, don't worry, you'll have plenty of time to be miserable with your team when you get back."

I decided to stay.

7.

The Chasm (Days 8–9)

Back in Washington, Pete Marocco, the newly appointed director of foreign assistance at the State Department, capitalized on the confusion surrounding the executive order to pursue his personal vendettas at USAID. Secretary Rubio had given Marocco full oversight authority over the agency. His hatred for the agency and its staff had been festering for years. Marocco had served a brief stint at USAID during the first Trump administration, but was pushed out after less than four months, following a memo filed by the agency's staff that accused him of severe mismanagement. Marocco, a former Marine Corps platoon sergeant, held the career staff responsible for his humiliating ouster, and the ensuing four years had done nothing to lessen his grudge. (Controversy followed Marocco during the intervening years. He was identified as one of the rioters who entered the U.S. Capitol on January 6, 2021.) Now he was back, overseeing USAID, and he had an axe to grind.

Even before Rubio issued his guidance to clarify the executive order, Marocco was convinced that the civil service was working to undermine the order by allowing payments to contractors after Trump had imposed the freeze. He demanded that the individuals responsible for subverting the will of the president be identified and removed. In reality, the civil service had taken extra precautions to avoid this precise scenario. Erring on the side of extreme caution, they had frozen all funds preemptively, even as they awaited guidance to clarify whether the order applied to existing programs in addition to new ones. The only payments that moved after January 20 were those that had been approved during the prior administration for work completed and invoiced before the executive order. Even if the order applied to these prior payments—and there was nothing in Trump's directive suggesting that was the case—USAID staff did not have the authority to freeze those payments, which were made automatically by financial payment systems managed by the Treasury Department. Marocco was either confused or lying.

Unsatisfied by the explanations he was hearing from Jason Gray and the political appointees at USAID, Marocco pressed forward with his accusations and his demands for retribution. On Monday, January 27, he arrived at the Reagan Building to investigate his claims of subversion. Accompanying him were Luke Farritor, a twenty-three-year-old coder and former SpaceX intern; Clayton Cromer, a former corporate attorney with ties to Trump's former U.S. attorney for the District of Columbia; and Edward "Big Balls" Coristine, a nineteen-year-old fresh out of high school and known primarily by his juvenile LinkedIn username.

These were not trained investigators; they were with DOGE, and Marocco had apparently put them in charge. The newcomers were given access to the agency's financial records, but rejected offers from career officials to help interpret them in the context of USAID operations. After a few hours, without ever meeting with the career staff, the DOGE team had identified their suspects: fifty-eight of the agency's most senior career officials. Although they provided no evidence linking the accused staff to the alleged violation—most of the individuals did not have any role in payment actions—the DOGE team directed Jason to place the officials on administrative leave.

That same evening, just one week after Trump's inauguration, Ramona called me again. If she'd been having a bad day the first time she called, this time was exponentially worse. She was calling me from Target, where she was shopping with her two children. I took the call from a stairwell, ducking out of my room immediately upon hearing the sound of Ramona's voice. I could tell this was not going to be a conversation that I wanted Steve listening in on.

Ramona jumped right in. At four thirty that afternoon, with no warning or explanation, Julie Wallace and her three deputies, along with fifty-four other senior leaders at USAID, had been placed on leave, removed from the building, and stripped of access to their email and all other agency systems. Ramona had sat with Julie in her office for those painful last few minutes as Julie relayed her final instructions and packed up her few personal items, before they both finally broke down in tears. The remaining staff were left shocked, confused, afraid, and uncertain of who was in charge. They didn't know who they were allowed to talk to, or what they were allowed to say.

This would have been an unprecedented challenge in the most stable of times, but now, with all our programs on hold, the GH Bureau suddenly confronted a complete leadership vacuum at the worst possible moment. But wait, Ramona told me as she aimlessly paced the aisles of Target, there was more.

We had not only lost our senior leadership that day; we had lost almost half of our staff as well. All of GH's contractor staff—the 374 GH staffers who were employed through a third-party contractor rather than directly by the government—had been fired. Due to the stop-work order, the contractor that had hired them had no way to pay their salaries and responded by terminating all their employees, effective immediately. Suddenly, hundreds of my colleagues had lost their jobs and were sent home without warning. While the executive order halting foreign assistance had been portrayed as a temporary pause to allow time to review our programs, the stop-work orders were already having a permanent impact.

I struggled to process what I was hearing. In one day, nearly half the global health workforce had been wiped out, including not only our senior leadership but also many of our core technical teams—doctors, epidemiologists, public health experts—whose expertise was irreplaceable. Adding to the confusion, we had lost every one of our administrative and program assistants across the bureau—all of whom were among the fired contractors—leaving us without the managers of our schedules, trackers, clearances, or communication channels.

I was shocked. I have no recollection of getting off the phone. I can only remember sitting in the stairwell trying to make sense of what Ramona had told me. I didn't know how the GH Bureau would even begin to function without the staff we had just lost. At the same time, unless we were able to restart our programs quickly, lives around the world would soon be at risk, if they weren't already. Then I thought about the lives of my colleagues who had lost their jobs. They had gone to work that morning with their top concern being the need to restart USAID's health programs. Now they were heading home without an income, some without health insurance for themselves and their families.

I returned to my room and called Julie. She sounded pissed off and tired, but I did not detect even a hint of resignation. "It's total bullshit," she said. "They're saying we were sneaking funds to circumvent the EO, even though the financial records prove that didn't happen."

Despite being unfairly removed from her job just a few hours earlier, she was already organizing the group of fifty-eight ousted officials. It was unclear how long they could be legally kept on administrative leave without being reinstated or formally disciplined, so they needed to quickly prepare their defense. "They'll have to provide some evidence soon, and we're already working on our response. I don't know what's coming next, but we're not quitting without a fight."

I had called thinking that I would be offering my condolences to a grieving colleague, but I quickly realized that this was not what Julie needed. Instead, amazingly, given the circumstances, the call turned into a chance for *me* to tap into *her* strength. I told her how horrible I felt that this had happened to her and that I had not been present to offer support.

"I appreciate you saying that, but there was nothing you could have done," she said. "It's actually probably better that you aren't here so they can't target you as well. But you're going to have to be careful when you get back. They're looking for any excuse to get rid of people at this point.

Don't give them one." By the end of the brief call, I felt more grounded. If she wasn't giving up, then I sure as hell couldn't either.

As I hung up, Steve came into the room and asked what was wrong. He had been walking on eggshells around me all week, recognizing that the presidential candidate he had been trumpeting all fall and winter was now wreaking havoc on the agency where I worked. Steve and I had been through a lot together over the years, but our long-standing friendship was strained. The few times we had broached the topic of the executive order pausing foreign assistance, the conversation had ended in a stalemate. I described the many ways that abruptly halting foreign aid was putting lives at risk. He countered that if it was as catastrophic as I made it sound then there would surely be exceptions to allow things like food and medicine to continue to flow. I explained that it was not so simple. Contracts were frozen, nothing was moving, and people would start suffering soon if they hadn't already. He simply did not believe that Donald Trump would let that happen.

Now I recounted to Steve what was happening back in Washington. I don't think I actually said, "I hope you're happy," but I have no doubt the tone was in my voice. Steve said he was sorry this was happening to my colleagues. "I don't want *you* to lose *your* job," he said. "The government needs good people like you. But there are some people who do need to lose their jobs. The government has gotten way too big, and no one even knows what they're doing anymore. . . ." He trailed off, realizing from my facial expression that I did not want to hear it right then, and left the room.

Suddenly, the entire mission of my agency felt extremely tenuous. Hundreds of our staff were gone, all our work was on hold, our leadership had been cut off, and I had no clear sense of what would come next. I realized I had waited too long—I couldn't believe how quickly the situation had deteriorated—and it was past time for me to get back to Washington.

The next day, Tuesday, January 28, with my return flight booked for the following morning, I was still thinking about my call with Julie, how impressively she had demonstrated calmness and strength. I had no idea how GH was going to function without her leadership, especially at a time like this. I was taking stock of which leaders remained in the bureau, wondering if there was anyone who could step in to fill the chasm left by Julie's removal, when a text message popped up on my phone from Alyssa, GH's budget director.

"Congrats?!? ☺ " it read.

I felt my stomach drop to my toes as I checked my email.

8.

Under Siege (Days 9–11)

In my inbox was an announcement from Jason Gray. It had gone out to the agency's entire workforce under the subject line "Leadership in USAID Bureaus and Independent Offices." New leaders had been designated for each of the bureaus, replacing the career leaders who had been pushed to administrative leave the previous day. And there, for GH, it read "Nicholas Enrich, Acting Assistant Administrator."

I did a double take, making sure I was reading correctly that I had just been assigned to lead all of USAID's global health efforts. My head spun, and I felt my throat starting to close. Why did they pick me? Was it a mistake? Surely someone would have at least called or texted to give me a heads-up before blasting the news out to the agency's ten thousand–plus staff. What if I didn't want the job? To be clear: *I really, really did not want the job.* I was absolutely not qualified to lead USAID's largest development sector and its team of eight hundred health experts. I was a program office director, the epitome of middle management. The last person to hold this position was the legendary Atul Gawande, for fuck's sake. Even if I had been qualified, being responsible for global health at a time when it was so squarely in the crosshairs was a frightening proposition. Would I be asked to sign off on actions that would result in thousands of people dying? What if I refused? Would I be fired? No, this had to be a mistake.

I found Jason's phone number in the directory, but as I started to dial, I hesitated. I had never called a USAID administrator before. Was I even allowed to do that? Maybe there was a protocol and I was supposed to call his assistant, or chief of staff, or executive secretary, or someone? I decided it didn't matter, I needed to try. I had worked with Jason a couple years earlier, when he was the agency's chief information officer. I remember he had a warm smile and was always eager to help find solutions. So I called him, and to my surprise he answered. Jason sounded nervous and reserved, speaking haltingly, in measured and calculated talking points, nothing like in our previous interactions.

The announcement was not a mistake, he said. I was now the top global health official at USAID. He could not tell me anything about why Julie Wallace and the others had been placed on administrative leave, only that it did not mean, necessarily, that they had done something wrong. All he would say was that changes were coming for the agency, and that I would learn more soon. I told him that I was currently in Canada, but that I was on my way home. I thanked him for taking my call and told him, with something less than full sincerity, that I looked forward to working with him.

That same day, there was another update, one that was far more promising than my new, unwelcome designation. Eight days after Trump's order freezing all foreign assistance, Rubio issued a memo titled "Emergency Humanitarian Waiver to Foreign Assistance Pause." The waiver specified that "implementers of lifesaving humanitarian assistance programs should continue or resume work if they have stopped." It went on to define what lifesaving meant: "core lifesaving medicine, medical services, food, shelter, and subsistence assistance, as well as supplies and reasonable administrative costs as necessary to deliver such assistance."

This was huge. It meant that USAID could restart many of the most critical health programs that had been frozen by the executive order. Clinics could reopen. Patients could once again access treatment for deadly diseases. After a week of devastation, Rubio's waiver gave me a glimmer of hope that the value of human life would not be completely abandoned as the president moved forward with the America First agenda. I wondered if Steve had been right. Even if the new administration was skeptical of foreign aid as a tool of diplomacy or national security, the waiver was a sign that it surely did not intend, without warning, to shutter neonatal clinics serving mothers and babies in urgent need of care, interrupt clinical trials by kicking patients off treatment for deadly diseases, or stop the world's most successful immunization campaign in its tracks.

With USAID's programs on indefinite hold across the globe, the entire foreign aid sector felt like a ticking time bomb that could go off at any minute, but now we had a chance to defuse it, at least for our lifesaving work. But we needed to act quickly. Every day we waited would put more lives at risk. Further, the window for restarting frozen activities was closing. We did not know how much time we had before more contractors took drastic action in response to having lost their funding. If contractors laid off their staff before we could indicate that their programs could continue under the waiver, it could take months, or even years, for them to effectively resume their work. As promising as the waiver was, we still faced significant challenges in implementing it. Not only had we lost half our staff, but we were still prohibited from communicating with anyone outside the agency. How could we tell our contractors to restart their work if we couldn't talk to them? We needed direction from our agency leaders, and they were apparently still hiding from us.

In the airport the next morning, I was preparing for a videoconference with the GH senior management team, which I had scheduled to hold before my flight boarded. This was the first time since my promotion that I would be speaking to the two dozen most senior officials in the bureau. But first I needed to talk to Nida Parks, GH's chief of staff. My goal for the staff meeting was to jump right in on implementing the waiver, and I wanted to get Nida's take.

As I saw it, with all our other programs still frozen, restarting lifesaving activities was the bureau's number one priority. My plan was simple: We would take the exact language from the waiver, send it to all our partners, and tell them to resume necessary activities. I knew we faced hurdles. There was the communications ban, and contractors would want more detailed guidance on what counted as lifesaving. But my feeling was that we needed to send the language out now and we could work out the details later. Nida agreed, as I suspected she would.

Tall, with bright blond hair, Nida was hard to miss in a meeting. And that was even before she started to speak. In an office culture that emphasized deference, conciliation, and consensus building, Nida was a bull in a china shop. She did not compromise on getting things right, and when she disagreed with someone, they were going to hear it. She would try to wait her turn in a meeting, but she could get antsy. If a speaker droned on too long, Nida's hand would shoot up in the air, like an eager freshman in a lecture hall. And when she spoke, it was with the conviction and clarity of someone who knew she was right, which she usually was. She was not afraid to upend assumptions in a roomful of senior officials or political appointees, and she could always be counted on to say the thing that no one else dared, even if everyone else was thinking it.

My inaugural meeting with the senior management team did not go as well as I had hoped. Not everyone saw things as clear-cut as Nida and I did. The director of the Office of HIV/AIDS was the first to burst my bubble, stating that we should not get ahead of the rest of the agency on issuing guidance to contractors. An attorney from general counsel added that contractors would need more detailed definitions of what counted as lifesaving and what did not, otherwise the scope of what they were allowed to do would be unclear.

I argued that we could work on refining the definition, but before that was ready we needed to tell the contractors to get back to work. After all, the waiver had already been issued, and it stated that implementers should resume work if they had stopped, which ours had. The firing of the 374 contractor staff who worked at GH was a cautionary tale. The waiver allowed for administrative expenditures necessary to deliver lifesaving assistance. In my reading, that meant that we could have told the staffing contractor to resume paying salaries for those workers who were needed to implement our lifesaving programs. Only, now they had all been fired, and it was too late. This was why we had to act now, before other contractors followed suit and took irreversible measures that would prevent them from restarting their work under the waiver.

Another office director argued that it would be too risky for GH to act on the waiver before we received authorization from the agency's political leadership, a not-so-subtle allusion to the fifty-eight senior staff who had just been placed on administrative leave for their alleged subversion two days earlier. I shot back that any of us could be ousted at any time, but we couldn't let that stop us from doing our jobs.

In the end, we settled on a compromise: Ramona, as my deputy, would attend a meeting that afternoon with USAID's new chief of staff, Joel Borkert, and would seek his approval before moving forward with implementing the waiver. Signing off from the call, I was discouraged. I knew that my colleagues were only trying to protect me by advocating for the more cautious approach of waiting for political cover. Maybe I was being reckless. But, to date, waiting for guidance from USAID's new leadership had been an exercise in futility, and I had no reason to think that would change.

Before my flight took off, I had a call with Alyssa Jernigan, GH's budget director. She could tell I was frustrated. She reminded me that everyone was extremely cautious because of everything that had happened over the past week. It was easy for me to say we needed to act now, but I had not been there to watch as our senior leaders were escorted out of the building. The environment at the office was scary, and people were nervous. Alyssa was right, and her insight gave me something to think about as I boarded the plane. What would I be walking into when I got back to Washington? Would it even somewhat resemble the office atmosphere I had left, or had everything changed?

Not knowing what to expect, I tried to focus on the things I could control. I promised myself that, no matter what awaited me, I would not be intimidated. I had a job to do, and I would do it. I didn't know how long I would be leading GH, but if I were pushed out for trying to restart lifesaving activities, I would have to be okay with that.

As I flew, Ramona met with Joel Borkert, covering for me at the agency's first meeting of bureau heads since Trump's inauguration. Like Jason Gray the night before, Joel was light on details. He framed the meeting as a reset, with the newly established civil service leadership now in place. He acknowledged that there was a great deal of uncertainty surrounding USAID and its programs and offered to help with any challenges during this period of transition. He thanked the career staff for their flexibility and promised to provide more updates shortly.

Ramona caught up with Joel as he was leaving the room and requested guidance on how to implement Rubio's waiver for lifesaving humanitarian assistance, noting several examples of global health activities that hung in the balance. While he claimed to agree with the urgency of restarting lifesaving programs, Joel seemed surprised to hear that so many activities within global health might fall into the category of the waiver. He had no specific advice on how to proceed, so Ramona suggested that GH could write up and send him our proposal for how we would implement the waiver. He liked that idea, and promised to prioritize it when it reached his desk. Ramona's impression—our first of the agency's new political leadership—was optimistic. Joel came across as open to helping us resume our most critical programs, even if he did not seem to understand what those programs might be.

We were under no illusions. The waiver was not a silver bullet; it was barely even a Band-Aid. The administration had already signaled that it was not interested in USAID's development model. Even if we were able to restart some of the most urgent lifesaving activities in the short term, our programs would not succeed over time if we abandoned our commitment to helping developing countries strengthen their health systems. USAID was in trouble, but I could not worry about that now. There was a waiver for lifesaving activities, and we needed to move quickly.

I returned to an agency under siege. Our remaining staff was confused and scared. The atmosphere was hardly recognizable from the one I had left on the eve of Trump's inauguration. Gone was the low din of collaborative chatter and laughter that usually emanated from our open workspace, replaced by an eerie silence fueled by fear and mistrust that sometimes bordered on paranoia. One staff member spent all day eyeing a suspicious-looking croissant that had been mysteriously left on her desk, fearing that it might be poisoned, only to learn later that a colleague had dropped it off in a failed attempt to brighten her day.

Even internal meetings no longer felt like a safe space to share information. P3 was normally responsible for guiding GH on contract management, and in my absence Ramona had decided that someone needed to fill the internal void of information created by the communications ban and the stop-work orders. She called a meeting with GH project managers to share what little she knew and to try to address the rumors and confusion. A self-proclaimed data nerd, Ramona was more comfortable analyzing numbers on a spreadsheet than presenting to a crowded conference room. Whenever she had to speak publicly, she made sure she knew her topic inside and out and designed an orderly presentation, hoping to preempt any questions that might catch her off guard. "I know it sounds dorky, but I think in PowerPoint slides," Ramona told me the first time we met. With no slides, no guidance to fall back on, and no way to answer the questions she knew would be flying at her, this meeting was the exact opposite of her comfort zone.

The meeting was tense. Project managers were ravenous for information, and this was the first time someone had given them an opportunity to ask questions and voice their concerns. Ramona stuck to her talking points, unsatisfying as they were, knowing that the slightest slip of a personal opinion could get back to leadership and get her in trouble. She covered the stop-work orders and what had been conveyed to contractors, reminded staff of the moratorium on communications, and provided what little information she had. She took questions, and while she did not have answers, she promised to elevate them to leadership. Then she ended the meeting.

But someone had secretly recorded the meeting and leaked the recording to the press. Within hours, Devex, a media outlet focused on international development, published an article titled "Don't Email Us, We've Got Very Few Answers, USAID Staff Told." The story quoted a "senior official who led the meeting" describing the situation as "a really crazy moment" and saying, "We want to be very, very careful about what we're putting in writing." Ramona felt betrayed by her colleagues, and now she was worried that she could be targeted. Those quotes might be perceived as her being sneaky or insubordinate.

I tried to reassure her. "The good news is, it could have been so much worse," I told her. "You must have done a great job if those were the juiciest quotes they came up with." But I was worried, too. After the DEI staff had been fired and the senior officials placed on administrative leave for simply doing their jobs, was it really out of the question that the new USAID leadership would retaliate against Ramona?

With our programs and staff on the ropes, DOGE and the political appointees launched a targeted attack against USAID's reputation for efficient, high-impact investments. DOGE had come in to make cuts, and their plan was to justify those cuts by demonstrating how wasteful our programs were. It was unclear how they were trying to find out which programs were wasteful—they certainly never asked the agency's staff. But it soon became clear that if they didn't find what they were looking for, they were happy simply to make up examples that would have been wasteful had they been real.

"We identified and stopped $50 million being sent to Gaza to buy condoms for Hamas," Trump announced from his podium at the White House on January 29. "And do you know what's happened to them? They've used them as a method of making bombs. How about that?"

How about that? If that were true, it certainly would have been a horrible waste of U.S. taxpayer funds, and I would have been furious to learn that my taxes were contributing to such a boondoggle. But of course, nothing about the president's statement was true. Leaving aside the head-scratching assertion that Hamas was somehow using condoms to make bombs, USAID had not sent any money to Gaza for condoms at all, let alone to Hamas. In fact, DOGE had mixed up their Gazas in their hurried quest to identify waste. The Gaza that had received the aid in question was Gaza Province in Mozambique, in southern Africa, not the Gaza Strip in the Middle East. And the funds were not simply for condoms, but for a comprehensive reproductive health package, including birth control, family planning counseling, and health education and awareness campaigns.

My colleagues and I watched, slack-jawed, as Trump delivered his blatantly false statement. Not because we were curious about how Hamas had built bombs with condoms they hadn't received, but because we had already warned our political leaders that this example of "waste" was not what DOGE was claiming it was.

At her first official media briefing on January 28, the White House press secretary, Karoline Leavitt, had highlighted the condoms-to-Gaza example as "a preposterous waste of taxpayer money." Her statement sent the USAID staff into a frenzied scramble to figure out what she was talking about. With no hints from DOGE about how they had "found" the Gaza condoms activity, GH staff pored through every project file, work plan, and financial report in a desperate search to uncover the error. Had we, somehow, unbeknownst to the health team or the regional bureau, accidentally sent $50 million for condoms to the Gaza Strip? It did not sound plausible, but we needed to make sure.

Once the source of confusion was identified, the team immediately informed Laken Rapier, USAID's political appointee for public relations, of DOGE's mistake. She was no doubt fielding an influx of media and congressional inquiries on what truly did sound like a horrendous investment, and she needed to be armed with the facts so she could help set the record straight.

But now, hearing Trump amplify the false assertion again the next day, we realized that Rapier had apparently sat on the response. For the first time, it began to dawn on me that our own agency's political appointees were not trying to support USAID. Instead, it seemed that they actually wanted the agency to look wasteful and for the staff to look incompetent, or worse.

9

Beyond Repair (Days 12–14)

With each passing day, the pressure continued to build. I reminded my senior staff that our top priority was to implement the waiver to restart lifesaving activities, and by Friday, January 31, we had drafted a memo with our refined definition of what constituted "lifesaving" support as well as a process we had devised to implement the waiver. As I waited for our technical teams to finalize their review, and for sign-off from our legal advisors, I emailed Joel Borkert, USAID's chief of staff, to summarize our approach, and to seek his approval to begin restarting key programs.

Joel didn't respond. The agency's political leadership did not share my top priority. At Pete Marocco's urging, DOGE was pushing for the permanent removal of the fifty-eight senior officials who had been placed on administrative leave. Similar to their search for waste within the agency, the DOGE team's investigation into whether the career staff had violated Trump's executive order by allowing payments to proceed was both cursory and preordained. Self-sequestered in an office in the Reagan Building, DOGE intentionally cut themselves off from the career staff who understood the complex financial reports they were reviewing. Had they asked the staff to help them interpret the documents, they would have learned that the records showing funds flowing after January 20 were not newly authorized expenditures, but previously approved, automatic payments for costs incurred during the Biden administration. Instead, career officials were left to nervously watch the colorful sneakers of the

DOGE team beneath the clouded-glass windows in the executive suite, unsure of how the inexperienced interlopers might interpret the nuanced financial data, but knowing that their senior leaders' fates might be decided in that room.

Luke Farritor, the twenty-three-year-old techie, relying on his own uninformed and contextless review of the agency's financial records, emailed his DOGE colleagues his conclusion that the fifty-eight senior officials had subverted the president's order (although he hedged that "I could be wrong . . . my numbers may be off"). It was unclear how the blame was assigned; even if there had been malfeasance, there was nothing in the reports that could have linked financial transactions to the accused officials. Still without any actual evidence, between Farritor's review and Marocco's conviction, the DOGE team figured they had what they needed. DOGE's new leader, Jeremy Lewin, a slick-talking twenty-seven-year-old Harvard Law School graduate, demanded that Jason Gray terminate the accused staff.

Nick Gottlieb, USAID's director of employee and labor relations, would have to sign off on the terminations. He refused. Nick, a trained attorney with more than seventeen years' experience handling employee relations for the federal government, wrote a memo to Jason in which he stated that "there is no evidence any of them attempted to circumvent the president's orders" and warned that DOGE's order to fire the staff was illegal.

Nick then wrote to the fifty-eight officials and informed them that "the materials show no evidence that you engaged in misconduct. As a result, I no longer have authority to maintain you in this status. . . . You may receive another email within the day reinstating your leave status. However, that notice will not come from me."

Nick's attempt to release the officials from administrative leave was his final official act. Just after 4 p.m. that day, he wrote another email, his last from a USAID account. Under the subject line "Illegal Activity in the USAID Front Office," Nick informed all agency staff that he, too, had now been placed on administrative leave, for refusing an illegal order to terminate staff without cause. "It is and has always been my office's commitment to the workforce that we ensure all employees receive their due process in any of our actions," he wrote. "I will not be party to a violation of that commitment."

The question of how civil servants would respond if they were directed to take improper or illegal actions was no longer hypothetical. The next test came within hours.

Nick's refusal to terminate staff without due process infuriated the DOGErs, who considered the incident another example of insubordination by USAID's career staff. They responded by seeking unprecedented access to sensitive USAID computer systems—and even for the authority to lock the agency's staff out of those systems—purportedly to uncover additional waste. The tech-minded DOGE team had determined that if they couldn't fire the staff, the next best thing would be to shut them out of their USAID email and other electronic systems.

Jason pushed back forcefully, arguing that shutting out the staff in this way could jeopardize the safety and even the lives of thousands of USAID workers stationed in unstable environments overseas. The pressure on him came from the highest levels, including Pete Marocco and Jeremy Lewin, two figures known to have zero patience for being challenged. Unlucky civil servants had directly observed Marocco's tirades at USAID during the first Trump administration. Jeremy was new to the agency, but an article in *Rolling Stone* portrayed him as being prone to "violent outbursts." It described several concerning incidents—including one where he allegedly threatened a woman with a kitchen knife, and another where he allegedly attacked a classmate with a bowl, giving him a bloody nose—a pattern so common that his classmates coined the label "#AngryLewin" as shorthand for his volatility.

Still, Jason refused to back down. Jeremy even called in Elon Musk to try to convince Jason to give in, but again, he would not budge. Enraged, the political appointees removed Jason's designation as acting administrator; he was relegated to his previous role as chief information officer, although the agency staff was not informed of his removal until the following week.

On Saturday, February 1, DOGE arrived at the Reagan Building, demanding access to USAID's most restricted space. The sensitive compartmented information facility, or SCIF, is a secure area that protects the agency's most guarded classified information, and access is heavily restricted. USAID security officers, confirming that DOGE staff did not have authorization to enter the restricted area, refused access in accordance with agency and government-wide national security protocols. The DOGE team protested, and John Voorhees, USAID's director of security, and Brian McGill, his deputy, were summoned to de-escalate the conflict. Voorhees, a former military policy commander and U.S. Army criminal investigator, explained to the DOGE team that their badges did not indicate a security clearance level sufficient to access the SCIF. Calls were made to DOGE and to the political leadership at USAID and State, but Voorhees held firm. He had no choice but to deny access to a secure facility unless the individuals had the required security clearance. By the end of the day, however, Voorhees and McGill had been shunted to administrative leave, and the DOGE team had gained full access to the SCIF and USAID's most sensitive systems.

Over that first weekend in February, as news spread about Nick Gottlieb, John Voorhees, and Brian McGill being placed on administrative leave for refusing to carry out illegal orders, and Jason Gray's ouster as acting administrator, I talked with Jordanna about the mayhem unfolding at work. I was unsettled by what had happened over the past few days. These were some of our most senior remaining career officials at USAID, and now their tenure at the agency was likely over because they had insisted on enforcing the law and USAID's rules. But I was also proud of how they had represented the civil service, implementing the policy directives of the administration, but refusing to obey unlawful orders, even if it meant putting their jobs at risk.

Jordanna asked if I would have done the same thing in their situation. I liked to think that I would have, but we both recognized that it was much easier to say so after the fact than in the heat of the moment, with Pete Marocco or Elon Musk demanding that you capitulate. Jordanna suggested that I start compiling a list of things that I could potentially be asked to do that would cross the line for me. That way I would be less likely to be caught off guard if and when it happened. On Sunday morning, February 2, I texted Julie Wallace (still on administrative leave) to check in. She had clearly been thinking about the same issue and responded: "Biggest advice is to not accept to do anything illegal. As those requests are coming."

In global health, illegal orders would likely look less cut-and-dried than those related to personnel or security rules. It might be more difficult to know whether a directive was a legitimate policy decision to carry out on behalf of the administration, even one I disagreed with personally, versus an illegal order. I anticipated that the most likely legal issues might relate to our appropriations from Congress. The executive order suggested that the administration would review which of our programs were in alignment with Trump's foreign policy agenda. What would happen if we were told not to pursue global health programs that had been specifically authorized and funded by Congress through legislation—for example, our earmarks for family planning or neglected tropical diseases? Appropriations law did not allow us to divert funds set aside for those purposes. What would I do if the political appointees directed us to not use those funds at all?

Another gray area was staffing. I was afraid that additional requests were coming to divide our staff into categories that would expose them to being fired or pushed to administrative leave, as had already happened to my colleagues who were working on DEI issues. I anticipated that this might come up again for additional categories like climate change or family planning. Would complying with those requests mean assisting with an illegal action? Certainly, placing more and more of our staff on the chopping block would make it impossible to effectively manage our programs, putting lives at risk around the world.

The administration's approach was unprecedented, but when I asked Julie for her advice, she was more cautious. Her take was that "the push of staff to admin leave based on EOs even if painful is not illegal—without cause—and I would do." This did not sit well with me. Admittedly, I was no human resources expert, but surely some justification was needed to place career staff on leave. Especially now, as it became clear that DOGE was using administrative leave as a tool to permanently remove individuals, what would I do when they came to me asking for names? I was still unsure, and I hoped that this situation would not come up again.

Through the weekend, the situation continued to deteriorate. Obviously furious that DOGE had been thwarted from its initial attempts to infiltrate USAID's systems and fire its staff, Musk turned to his mega-megaphone, X, and spent the weekend trashing USAID to his hundreds of millions of followers. He tweeted obsessively about USAID all Saturday night, including forty-nine posts between three and four o'clock on Sunday morning. The messages varied, including everything from amplifying content from Mike Benz and other conspiracy theorists to reposting a tweet from Senator Rand Paul calling on the Trump administration to "abolish USAID and all foreign aid."

Perhaps he went to sleep after that, as the barrage let up for a bit. But Musk's vilification of USAID picked back up as the clock struck noon on Sunday.

At 12:04 p.m. he reposted a message from Benz, adding: "USAID was a viper's nest of radical-left marxists who hate America."

At 12:06, he tweeted simply: "USAID is evil."

At 12:20, responding to a tweet describing how John Voorhees and Brian McGill had tried to prevent the DOGE team from accessing the SCIF: "USAID is a criminal organization. Time for it to die."

At 12:54, sharing a teaser from Benz about his plans to continue exposing USAID as a CIA front: "USAID is a criminal organization."

At 2:06 he asked his followers: "Did you know that USAID, using YOUR tax dollars, funded bioweapon research, including COVID-19, that killed millions of people?"

The baseless attacks continued throughout the afternoon and evening. In a live session Sunday night, Musk colorfully described his impression of USAID to his viewers: "It became apparent that what we have here is not an apple with a worm in it, what we have actually, just a ball of worms. You've got to basically get rid of the whole thing. . . . It's beyond repair."

At a little after 9 p.m., Trump piled on, telling reporters on live television that "USAID is run by radical lunatics and we're getting them out."

By late Sunday afternoon, my colleagues had begun to reach out to me, to express concern about whether Musk's rant might have real-world consequences. Was it safe for them to come to the office on Monday? Some of my colleagues felt as if they had become targets, worrying that they might be harassed or attacked by an emboldened Trump supporter eager to root out the "criminals" and "lunatics" at USAID. Was extra security needed at the office? If so, with the leadership of the security office having been removed, who would oversee any new security protocols? My advice was for everyone to plan to come into the office on Monday unless they were instructed otherwise. I hoped these concerns would prove unfounded, but it was not a pleasant thing to have to consider on the morning commute.

Far more worrisome than a flurry of angry tweets, I learned on Sunday afternoon that the Ministry of Health in Uganda had just reported an outbreak of Ebola. The initial case, a thirty-two-year-old healthcare worker, had initially sought treatment in at least three health facilities in the capital city, Kampala, as well as from a traditional healer, before succumbing to the lethal virus. Tests subsequently confirmed that the illness was indeed Ebola, and the Ugandan Ministry of Health had identified hundreds of potential close contacts for follow-up, as well as alerting the World Health Organization and the U.S. Centers for Disease Control and Prevention.

If I needed any reminder that I was unqualified to lead global health for USAID, this was a stark one. An Ebola outbreak anywhere in the world is considered a high-level national security concern for the United States. The government's response is coordinated by the National Security Council, and USAID plays a central role during an outbreak in coordinating international partners and providing emergency funding, logistics, technical assistance, and health systems support. As acting assistant administrator, the responsibility fell on me to lead the agency's response, representing USAID at the NSC for the duration of the outbreak. As with any infectious disease outbreak, speed was critical.

Establishing an immediate and robust response was the best chance to prevent the disease from spreading unchecked in Uganda—and thus prevent its spread to other countries. I had exactly zero experience in responding to Ebola outbreaks, nor had I ever engaged directly with the NSC. Luckily, I would be supported by our Outbreak Response Team, which was already preparing our plan of attack. But they had already lost several key staff members due to the terminations the previous week. We set a meeting for Monday morning to walk through the plan.

That night I lay in bed, bone-tired but wired awake, restlessly flashing through ever more dire scenarios of what the coming week might bring. It was the worst case of the Sunday scaries I can remember in my life.

PART TWO

SAWDUST

10.

Access Denied (Day 15)

Sometime in the early hours of Monday, February 3, DOGE changed its plans for USAID—and its tactics. Elon Musk and his team were no longer interested in eliminating waste within the agency; they now decided to destroy it entirely. If there were any doubts as to Musk's intentions, he clarified them in a tweet at 1:54 a.m.: "We spent the weekend feeding USAID into the wood chipper. Could gone [*sic*] to some great parties. Did that instead."

After axing John Voorhees and Brian McGill over the weekend, DOGE took advantage of its newly unfettered access to USAID's classified systems and restricted areas. They granted themselves root access to USAID email and computer systems, allowing them to do anything from spamming the entire workforce to disabling user access on a whim. And they went straight to work on chopping up the agency.

The USAID website, USAID.gov, which detailed all the programs, lessons, and results of American foreign aid over the past six decades, was shut down, erasing the official repository of the agency's rules, data, and policies. Gavin Kliger, a twenty-six-year-old software engineer turned DOGE operative, tapped into the agency's emergency notification system and blasted out an ominous message agency-wide:

At the direction of Agency leadership, the USAID headquarters at the Ronald Reagan building in Washington, D.C. will be closed to Agency personnel on Monday, February 3, 2025. Agency personnel normally assigned to work at USAID headquarters will work remotely tomorrow, with the exception of personnel with essential on-site and building maintenance functions individually contacted by senior leadership. All staff working in all other NCR [National Capital Region] facilities will come in as usual. Further guidance will be forthcoming.

In light of the events of the past few days, the abrupt closure of USAID's headquarters building was a bad sign, although it did not appear to apply directly to GH, as we were located in the USAID Annex building in L'Enfant Plaza, not the Reagan Building on Pennsylvania Avenue. Still, DOGE's midnight missive was sure to add to the confusion and concern already spreading. With Musk's announcement of the shredding of the agency an hour later, my colleagues woke up Monday morning in a full-fledged panic.

I arrived at the office at 7 a.m. Given the cryptic overnight message announcing the closure of USAID headquarters, I did not know what to expect when I entered the Annex building. I opened the door and stepped out of the predawn twilight into the lobby, half expecting the security guards to turn me away. Even though I had done this walk a thousand times before, that morning I felt like a spy behind enemy lines, holding my breath as I passed through the turnstiles, then speed-walking to the elevators and pushing the DOOR CLOSE button as soon as I got on, before security could change their minds and tell me to leave.

Seven o'clock was earlier than I usually got to work, but it was going to be a busy day and I needed some time to collect my thoughts. At 7:17, Julie Wallace texted: "The news is reporting no one should go into the office—closed today! It is over. Awful." I didn't believe it was over just yet, but I knew I had my work cut out for me. As the first rays of sunlight crept across the cubicles outside my office on the seventh floor, I tried to develop a manageable plan of attack for the day.

Our work and our staff were on the ropes. All our programs were on hold, and cracks were starting to show; project managers still had not responded to the repeated warnings from our in-country partners about their inability to operate and the impact it was already starting to have on their work. I urgently needed to find a way to convince our political appointees—whom I still hadn't met—to let us restart critical projects under Rubio's waiver for lifesaving assistance. On top of all that, there was that Ebola outbreak.

There were urgent morale concerns as well. Everyone at USAID was confused and afraid. Half the GH workforce had been fired or placed on administrative leave within the past week. Those of us who remained were desperate for guidance, direction, reassurance, anything. And Musk tweeting vitriol about our agency at bot-like frequency was not helping. It was not clear how we could withstand the wanton attacks from DOGE and at the same time do our jobs. Something had to give.

By eight o'clock, I had my to-do list ready. I would hold a senior management team meeting at nine to ensure that my top lieutenants were aligned on our priorities, which were: (1) find a way to implement the lifesaving humanitarian assistance waiver to restart our most crucial services, and (2) improve our communications with our teams within GH, which had broken down over the past several days. After the meeting, I would finalize the new guidance memo my team had drafted outlining the steps for resuming key programs. Then I would contact Joel Borkert, USAID's chief of staff, to get him to endorse our approach. Next, I would turn my attention to the Ebola outbreak. I needed a situation report from the remaining experts on our Outbreak Response Team, and then we were going to need the front office's help to effectively respond in spite of all the new restrictions imposed on our funding, travel, and communications. It was a daunting task, but I had seen the ORT at work before. Emergency logistics planning with constrained resources was their bread and butter, and I knew they were already pulling together options.

The morning schedule I had planned out wouldn't address all our problems—not even close. But this seemed like a reasonable way to dive in. I saw that several of my colleagues had begun to arrive for the day. I didn't see many smiling faces, but what I did see was a determination that reflected my own. All around the world, lives were on the line this morning, and I could plainly see that my team was not ready to give up. I felt a brief surge of optimism, thinking that we just might get through this.

And then chaos erupted.

At eight thirty, I received a chat message from a colleague who had just arrived at the office. The security guards had stopped her at the entrance and would not let her enter the building. This was concerning. The lack of direct communication from our political leadership, coupled with Musk's social media barrage, had us all on edge, and even the slightest anomaly felt like a five-alarm fire. But there had not been another email informing staff that our building was closed. Maybe there was a more benign explanation. Perhaps the guards had not let her in because she forgot her badge, or the turnstiles had malfunctioned. After all, I was already upstairs, as were several other staff members.

Then my phone rang, and the fears were confirmed. On the line was Alyssa Jernigan, calling from the front entrance. She described the scene that was unfolding downstairs. There was a crowd of staff in the lobby, all of whom had been denied entry. Security told them that the building was closed and that they should go home. Guards were purportedly on their way upstairs to locate and escort out any staff already inside the building. Before hanging up, Alyssa asked for a favor: "If you have time before you get kicked out, can you please grab the wedding photo from my desk?"

I was stunned. I called Jason Gray—mistakenly believing that he was still the acting administrator—but got no answer. I emailed him and Joel Borkert, urgently requesting that they allow my colleagues into the building. Then, feeling like a fugitive for the second time that morning, I poked my head out the door of my office and looked around. It was clear that my colleagues had heard the news as well. A few were crying, others were hurriedly gathering their belongings, and several were just standing in the hallway, unsure of what to do.

Suddenly, I remembered that I was supposed to be in charge. I had to say something, even though I had no idea what to do. Then I remembered

Alyssa's request, and realized that she had astutely identified the top priority. I had no way of knowing when, or if, we'd be allowed back in the building, and yet many of my colleagues had personal items at their workstations with untold sentimental value. If there was anything I could do to save those personal effects from being heartlessly discarded by DOGE, I needed to act now.

I gathered everyone within earshot and asked them to help. "Grab a bag, or a box, whatever you can find. Quick as you can, collect your personal items, and any of your colleagues'. We may be escorted out of the building at any time. Let's try to save anything we can." And off we went.

I rushed to Alyssa's office and found the framed photo of her and her husband on their wedding day. Then I sent a group message to my team, asking if anyone had items they wanted me to retrieve. For the next twenty minutes, I dashed about the office like a burglar on a heist, filling my tote bag with personal belongings—photos of families and pets, certificates of awards recognizing outstanding public service, a change of shoes—as I nervously watched the elevators for the approaching security guards who would force me to leave.

And then, as suddenly as the mayhem started, it was over. By nine o'clock, someone had instructed the security guards to reopen the building. By nine thirty, everyone had made it to their desks, and I had returned the last photo to its owner. I tried to regroup, rescheduled the senior management team meeting to ten o'clock, and made a note to remind everyone to take home their personal belongings at the end of the day—I did not want to go through the same exercise tomorrow. Clearly DOGE was trying to unnerve us, and I couldn't let it throw me off. We still had a lot to do.

Everyone was flustered at the 10 a.m. senior staff meeting. The norm in GH was for all meetings to start promptly at five minutes after the hour or half hour, but office directors and deputy directors staggered in at seemingly random intervals that morning, as they had prioritized spending time with their teams over punctuality. They looked as disheveled as I felt, some with tears in their eyes, others wearing their winter coats and carrying boxes or suitcases filled with their belongings in case we were kicked out again without warning. The scene was more appropriate for a train platform than an office conference room.

I realized that I needed to adjust my expectations for the meeting. One of the topics I had planned to cover was a recommendation to restrict meetings to in-person only. The debacle with Ramona's meeting the previous week, which had been recorded and sent to the press, was not the only example of videoconferences being recorded and then leaked, and it was making it even more difficult to communicate openly. But now this point seemed moot. After the morning's chaos, I had no idea how much longer any of us would be working in-person at all. I crossed that item off my agenda.

Instead, I shifted topics to Rubio's waiver, the one area where I felt we still had some degree of agency. Distracted as we all were, strategizing about how to get our programs back on track helped to sharpen our focus. I told the group that we needed teams to cut through the noise and prioritize restarting our lifesaving programs. Even those who had been hesitant the previous week had come around. Nida Parks, GH's chief of staff, walked through our process to finalize the memo for Joel Borkert's approval by the end of the day, with the goal of sending out instructions to contractors to restart activities by no later than Tuesday. Everyone agreed. The meeting ended with each office director tasked with taking stock of which of their programs met the definition of "lifesaving" so that we would be ready with a list of projects to resume, and as we exited the conference room, I was pleased to see our bureau's senior staff had more of a sense of purpose than when they walked in.

My next meeting was with the Outbreak Response Team. The National Security Council had contacted Joel Borkert, and he wanted to meet at noon to understand how GH would respond to the Ebola outbreak in Uganda. Having never led an outbreak response, I needed a briefing first. We met in Atul Gawande's old office on the seventh floor, and as the group of five or six filed into the room and sat down, no one sat in the chair that was somewhat larger than the rest—the one reserved for the assistant administrator. Megan Fotheringham, the deputy director of the Office of Infectious Diseases, who had served as a mentor to me for many years when

I worked on tuberculosis, now insisted that I sit in the big chair. After awkwardly demurring, I took the seat.

Despite the topic at hand—a lethal infectious disease outbreak—the meeting with the ORT was my first of the day where no one was panicking. Led by Travis Betz, a former logistician and operations director for the American Red Cross who then spent fifteen years working in humanitarian assistance and disaster relief at USAID, the ORT was built to function during a crisis. Travis and his team succinctly briefed me on the status of the outbreak, the key concerns and challenges, and the proposed next steps.

This outbreak was especially concerning, Travis said, given that it was based in Kampala, a metro area that was home to more than 6 million people—including ten thousand American citizens. Additionally, the first individual who got sick had traveled to several different medical clinics, including by public transportation. He was likely infectious during that period and had come in contact with a huge number of people, including many healthcare workers and at least a few Americans living in Kampala, who were now spreading across the city and its outskirts. These individuals needed to be identified and assessed for possible symptoms immediately.

"Having worked on many Ebola outbreaks," Travis warned, "this one could be very bad if we don't get on top of it quickly. And we're working with our hands tied behind our back."

Our biggest challenges were the new barriers that had been imposed since January 20. By this point in an outbreak, we would normally have a team of experts from Washington on the ground in Uganda to organize response efforts, and our contractors in the country would have already started mobilizing resources for contact tracing and infection control efforts. But none of these things had happened because of the executive order pausing foreign aid. Our contractors' activities were frozen by stop-work orders. The communications ban had prevented USAID from coordinating a response with partners in Uganda and at the global level, including the World Health Organization and UNICEF. Also, the ORT had lost several key technical experts when all of GH's contractor staff were fired, further reducing the team's ability to mount a rapid response. We needed to restart these key activities, lift the communications ban, and halt any further staff cuts so the team could get the response back on track.

As soon as that meeting ended, we all shuffled to the executive conference room down the hall—the freshly named Atul Gawande Conference Room—for the meeting with Joel Borkert and Paul Seong, who joined by video from the Reagan Building. It was my first time meeting Joel and Paul, a career foreign service officer who had recently been assigned as a senior advisor to the agency's front office. I was relieved to finally get some face time, even if only virtually.

Joel, who appeared to be in his mid- to late forties, with short reddish hair and a beard that was just starting to turn gray, told us that he needed to know what was happening with the Ebola outbreak and how he could help. I introduced myself and the team, and then I turned the floor over to Travis, who provided a version of the situational report that I had just heard, including the challenges that we faced. Joel told us that he had spoken to Pete Marocco, who we now learned was the new deputy administrator for USAID, and Joel's new boss. Marocco had made clear to him that the "changes" taking place at the agency were not to interfere with our response to the Ebola outbreak. "Anything you need," Joel said, "just let me know how I can help."

Encouraged, we gave him the list. We needed to instruct our contractors to restart activities in Uganda. We needed them to train and organize community health workers to conduct contact-tracing investigations to understand the extent of the outbreak. We needed them to initiate Ebola screening of outbound passengers at transportation hubs to ensure that the disease did not spread to other regions or countries. We needed to get personal protective equipment and other key supplies into the affected areas rapidly. We needed to reopen communications with our partners, and, most immediately, with the WHO. As part of our global health security strategy, USAID had already purchased twenty-seven thousand sets of personal protective equipment for a potential Ebola outbreak in the region, and they were sitting in a WHO-owned warehouse in Kenya. Reopening communications with the WHO would allow us to move the PPE into neighboring Uganda within hours.

And we needed our team to be able to focus on the problem. With the firing of our contractor staff, we had lost key Ebola experts and project managers. An Ebola outbreak is an all-hands-on-deck exercise, and the ORT usually pulls "crisis operations staff" from other teams to provide surge support. But the bureau had lost so much of its staff that ORT members were actually being pulled to help out on other diseases instead of being able to concentrate on the emergency. Joel appeared to grasp the severity of the situation. "Write it all up and send it to me, and I'll do everything I can," he promised.

Paul Seong had sat silently in Joel's office for the duration of the meeting. As soon as it ended, however, he sent me a chat message, asking for the names of the ORT staff who had been in the meeting. Paul's role in all of this was not clear, but he seemed to be the only career official in all of USAID who had the ear of our new political leaders. I knew that he had served in multiple roles throughout his career in the foreign service, including as a health officer at one point, so I hoped he could be helpful in explaining the value of USAID's global health programs. I definitely wanted him on our side. I did not know why taking attendance from the meeting was his priority, but I gave him the names, noting that there were others on the team that were contributing to the response but who had not attended the meeting.

Walking back to my office from the conference room, happy to have at least made initial—and somewhat promising—contact with our agency's leadership, I had a vague sense that something was different about the decor in the hallway. It felt emptier in a way I could not immediately put my finger on. When I got to my office, Natalia Machuca, the deputy director of human resources for GH, was waiting for me, agitated. Natalia was an ultramarathoner with a well-deserved reputation for perseverance in the face of daunting odds, which made what she said next especially concerning.

"We're being deleted," she said, and then showed me a photo from outside the Reagan Building. It showed a construction worker standing in the basket of a blue cherry picker, pulling the *A* from the word AGENCY off of the AGENCY FOR INTERNATIONAL DEVELOPMENT sign above the building's main entrance. DOGE had sent in a demolition crew to remove, letter by letter, USAID's name from our headquarters building. The message could not have been clearer.

Suddenly, I realized why the hallway had felt empty, and I ran back out of my office to confirm. The pictures that had decorated the hallway with images of all the progress USAID achieved around the world were gone. I looked into a conference room and saw the same thing. I walked down to the sixth floor, then the fifth. Everywhere I went, the picture frames—which until recently had held photos of USAID staff delivering bags of flour, of a doctor providing medicine to her patient, of a local community leader celebrating the opening of a new school—were empty. The demo crew had gone floor to floor, removing all evidence of our impact in the world.

At around three in the afternoon I retreated to my office to spend a few minutes scanning my inbox, braced for more bad news. My attention was immediately drawn to a State Department announcement that had been sent to the entire USAID workforce. Apparently, Jason Gray was out, and USAID had a new leader: "As an interim step toward gaining control and better understanding over the agency's activity, President Donald J. Trump appointed Secretary Marco Rubio as Acting Administrator."

As I was considering what this meant, the director of the Office of Population and Reproductive Health came into my office. She told me that several of her colleagues had just lost access to their email accounts. She had a list of those who were locked out, but explained that the problem seemed to be bureau-wide, with some entire teams across GH no longer able to access the USAID network. People were in tears, she told me, not sure if they had lost their jobs. Did I know what was going on? I told her I didn't, and I quickly refreshed my email to confirm it was still working. I was still online, but I wanted to understand how widespread the system outages were, and if there was any discernable pattern or explanation.

I left my office and bumped into Alyssa and Ramona, who were standing in the hallway with a few other staff members. Everyone looked bewildered, holding their coats and overstuffed bags packed with personal items.

They told me they had been digitally locked out. With everything that had already transpired that day, I had no doubt that this was something much more nefarious than an ordinary network outage. Still, it was hard to believe. These were among our most critical staff, and there was no way GH could function without them. Should they go home? If they did, would we ever see one another again? No one knew what to do, and I had no clue what to tell them. I asked them to give me an hour and I would find out what I could.

I sent a message to Joel, explaining what was happening. When I didn't hear back immediately, I called a GH senior staff meeting to try to figure out who was affected and what we should do. By then, nearly half the remaining staff in the bureau, including several entire offices, had lost access, and the problem was spreading. Multiple office directors learned that they had been locked out in real time during that meeting. While we met, another agency-wide emergency notification was delivered to those of us who still had system access. It was similar to the one sent early that morning, but broader. It informed us that all USAID facilities in the National Capital Region would be closed on Tuesday, and until further notice. This time, the USAID Annex was specifically referenced. We were barred from our office, starting tomorrow.

For how long? Was this really it? I looked around the room and saw the shock I was feeling reflected back at me in the eyes of my colleagues. A long silence followed, until I finally realized everyone was waiting for me to break it.

I didn't know what to say, but I was still not ready to give up. I started by saying that, while I did not know why access was being cut, we should not assume that it meant that those affected were being terminated. I explained that the agency's chief of staff had told me that the political leadership was committed to at least providing a robust response to the Ebola outbreak, which would be impossible if we were all locked out. I reasoned that there must be a misunderstanding somewhere along the chain. I told them I was going to leave this meeting and call everyone in the USAID front office until I found someone who would help me fix this.

In the meantime, I asked those who still had access to support the ORT to pull together the full outbreak response plan to be delivered to Joel later that afternoon. Nida passed around a sheet of notebook paper to collect personal emails so that everyone could stay connected even if they lost access. Someone—I can't remember who, but someone with much more compassion and situational awareness than I was able to invoke in that moment—suggested that those of us who had been cut off from the system spend the rest of the afternoon making the rounds in the office to speak with their team members who had lost access, letting them know that we care about them, and helping them in any way we can before they went home.

Hustling back to my office, I passed through a hallway in upheaval. Friends who had worked together for decades were crying and hugging, not knowing if or when they would see one another again. Professionals who had spent their entire adult lives trying to make the world a healthier place stared blankly, unsure of what they would be doing tomorrow, or forever. Was this really happening? Were we witnessing the complete disintegration of American foreign aid?

I called Joel again, and this time I reached him. As calmly as I could, I described the situation at the USAID Annex, trying to explain the implications in the terms we had discussed earlier in the day. "How can we stand up a response to the Ebola outbreak when our entire bureau is being kicked out of the system?" I asked in the least shaky voice I could muster.

Joel sounded frustrated—not as frustrated as I was, but not happy. He told me that the same thing was happening across the agency, without any input from the political leadership. It was DOGE, utilizing their new controls over USAID systems, who were removing access for huge swaths of the workforce. He said he had told DOGE that there were critical programs across the agency that would not be able to continue if the staff did not have access to email and systems, and he had mentioned the Ebola outbreak specifically.

He also told me that he had given DOGE a list of names of staff who would need to keep access in order to manage the Ebola response, so those individuals at least should still have access. I confirmed it was the same list of names I had given to Paul Seong earlier that afternoon. I was incredulous, telling Joel what I had told Paul, that those were only the names of the people who had been on the video call and would not be sufficient, on their own, to effectively manage the outbreak. He then asked me if I had a couple other names to add to the list who would allow for a more complete response.

I honestly did not know where to start. It was as if he had stripped all the parts from a car and now wanted to know if there were a few components I needed to make it run again. We needed the experts in laboratory and supply chain management. We needed the program managers, budget experts, data analysts, and procurement specialists to ensure the integrity, accountability, and efficacy of the work. We needed the country backstops who engage with the host government, as well as those of the surrounding countries. And that's just within GH. We also needed lawyers, contracting officers, financial controllers, legislative engagement officers, country desk officers, mission health officers, and many others who were housed in various offices across the agency.

And that was just for the Ebola outbreak in Uganda. What did this conversation mean for our other critical programs that remained in limbo, including so many that fell within the lifesaving humanitarian assistance waiver? Would we just abandon them without even closing them down? I stammered something about how just adding a few names would not be sufficient, that they needed to stop removing our staff until we were able to assess the critical functions and associated staffing needs to fulfill them.

Joel told me that turning system access back on for all staff was not realistic, and continued to push me for a list of specific individuals who were truly essential. "It's going to have to be draconian," he told me. I promised to get him a list as soon as possible, although I had no idea how I would put such a list together.

Around 5 p.m. I lost system access. I was standing in a common area on the seventh floor with the few ORT staff who remained online, frantically trying to finalize the various actions needed to move forward with the

Ebola outbreak response, when I was suddenly locked out of my email. I tried to log back in, but my credentials didn't work. I was out. I had been messaging a legal question to an attorney in general counsel when I lost access, and I now switched over to a colleague's laptop whose account was still active. I told the lawyer what had happened, and that now I was using someone else's computer to continue the discussion. She responded that I should not be using someone else's account if I had been locked out and refused to engage further.

At a complete loss, I told the team that Megan Fotheringham was in charge now. The deputy director of infectious diseases, who had assigned me the big chair in Atul's old office earlier that day, was the most senior staff member who still had access. I briefly made eye contact with Megan, but then she looked down and I turned away.

I called Joel yet again, and told him that I, too, had lost access. He sighed with exasperation—which, again, did not sound like it matched my own—and promised to get me turned back on. Then I stood around, watching the remaining few staff members continue to work, wondering what my role was, whether I still had a job, what would become of our staff or our work in the days and weeks to come. Eventually, the ORT finished the request for support on Ebola and Megan fired it off to Joel "on behalf of Nick." Unsure of what to do next, we gathered our remaining belongings, walked out into the early February darkness, hugged each other goodbye, and went our separate ways.

I arrived home feeling entirely defeated. I wanted to tell Jordanna about everything that happened that day, but I didn't know where to start. Not even a week earlier, I had been designated to lead a bureau of eight hundred people responsible for billions of dollars of programs that affected millions of lives around the world, and now I didn't even know how to get in touch with my staff. I had run around all day like my hair was on fire, and in the end I had accomplished nothing. I had been bouncing from one reaction to the next without even a hint of strategic thinking.

USAID was being demolished, on my watch, and I had done absolutely nothing to stop it.

Jordanna told me to slow down and breathe. I needed to put this in perspective. There was nothing I could have done to prevent this. Even the political appointees had been powerless to stop DOGE. Then she reminded me that all was not totally lost, at least not yet. If Joel was able to restore my access, I would have another chance. What would I do with it? Could I pull together a team that could come up with a plan to execute our most essential functions? Could I connect with the other bureau leaders to try to coordinate our efforts?

I thought I might be able to do it, if I had the right people to help me. I had lost my cool, intimidated—though I had promised myself I wouldn't be—by DOGE's onslaught. But I would not let it happen again. I just needed one more chance.

At 8 p.m., I checked my email again, and this time it was working. I sent a message to Joel, letting him know I was back online. His response was equal parts encouraging and infuriating:

DOGE is turning people off but in a very corporate way without mission critical analysis, then we come in and do the repairs. So I appreciate the help and patience. I wish there was a more respectful and deliberate way to do this, but it's out of my control. So I am extremely sorry for you and your hard working team.

I couldn't believe what he was telling me. Someone at DOGE was just flipping a switch to shut off access for staff across the agency, with no direction from any political appointee or any knowledgeable career staff, and with no regard for the impact it would have on our operations? As far as I could tell, the entire TB, malaria, and maternal and child health teams had been switched off, even as their lifesaving programs hung in the balance. Was DOGE really using no criteria whatsoever to determine who to shut off and who to keep?

Joel asked me for "a list of who you need, it needs to be lean and I'll see what I can do." I gave him a short list of the names of the people I would need to come up with a plan "that might allow us to avert total disaster on emergency lifesaving activities."

"Okay, I'll get them turned back on," he responded, adding: "Tomorrow I want you to come into the [Reagan Building] for a 30 min discussion on mission critical capabilities for the long term." I thought, but did not type, that it was insane to have the discussion of "mission critical capabilities" *after* all our staff had been jettisoned.

Apparently Joel's plan was to negotiate with DOGE to turn staff back on one by one, based on a list of names I would provide. Two weeks earlier our agency had been led by Samantha Power and Atul Gawande, who had insisted that we justify every action based on how it furthered our long-term strategic aims, and now a group of tech bros with no official positions or experience were pressing buttons like children playing in a toy spaceship. It was amazing how far off the rails we had fallen.

My blinders had finally been removed, and for the first time I was seeing unequivocally that USAID was facing an extinction event. I stared at the screen, reading Joel's message once more. Tomorrow I would have thirty minutes to convince our political leadership that USAID's global health programs were worth saving. I opened a blank document and began preparing for what I knew might be the most important presentation of my career.

11.

Grave Digging (Days 16–17)

With all of USAID's offices closed to staff, I worked from home on Tuesday, February 4, trying to find out what was left of the agency. It was a daunting task; most of my top subordinates in the Bureau for Global Health had lost access to their email and to USAID's electronic systems, which meant I couldn't even activate our emergency phone tree. I scanned the directory to find who might still be online. I pinged personal emails and cell phones. Although earlier in my career I had helped establish USAID's Critical Coordination Structure to ensure the agency's continuity of operations in the face of external threats or disruptions, I found myself completely unprepared for the scenario I faced that morning: The administration was intentionally shutting down USAID from within.

Joel Borkert emailed me to postpone that day's meeting to Wednesday, with no explanation. I was frustrated by the delay, but it felt like the least of my problems. I focused instead on trying to ascertain the status of the hundreds of people who should be working for GH, which felt like groping around in a dark cave without a flashlight. An email blast yielded dozens of error messages indicating failed delivery. As I scrolled through our internal staff directory, the extent of the problem became increasingly clear. I learned that when a USAID employee lost system access, his or her Gmail icon was removed—whether a professional headshot with the agency's flag in the background, a more casual picture depicting a hobby or a pet, or just initials—and replaced by a nondescript gray humanoid figure with a diagonal line through it, indicating the user's nonexistence. As I typed names into the directory, I was repeatedly greeted by this ghostly image of a colleague who used to be.

Somehow Natalia Machuca, GH's deputy director for human resources, was able to pull together a list of GH staff who remained, 151 in all. As she and I reviewed the list, trying to understand which teams and capacities were still online, it became obvious that there was no rhyme or reason to who had been cut and who remained. The surviving few were a patchwork of largely remote staff who were based outside of Washington, suggesting that DOGE had either failed to find them, or they were more difficult to disconnect than those who worked in the main office. There was also a seemingly random spattering of individuals from across the bureau's offices, with no discernable connection to one another. Many USAID employees no longer had a supervisor, and many supervisors had no staff left reporting to them.

Those who were online did reach out, to let me know they were still there and to see how they could help. Mostly they had questions. Several colleagues emailed me in tones that were just as scared and confused as the staff who had been removed, looking for answers as to why they were still online when their peers or supervisors were gone. In a way, the responses were as discouraging as the nonresponses from those who had lost access. I had no idea what to tell them. I didn't even know who many of them were, much less what they could do.

Once I had a sense of who was still online, my next question was about the status of the hundreds of individuals who had lost access. Joel had described them as having been "turned off," but obviously this was not an official employment status. They had received no notification that they were being placed on administrative leave. How could they? Without access to their email they would not have received the notification even if it had been sent. If they weren't on administrative leave, then where did that leave them? Was the outage temporary, in which case I should be pushing for them to be reconnected? Had they been fired?

I contacted the employment and labor relations office, where Nick Gottlieb had been the director until recently, for answers. But that email bounced back too; even USAID's human resources team had been locked out of the system. Joel had already told me that it was DOGE who was removing staff access, but I had assumed that what he meant was that DOGE was instructing HR to take action. It had not occurred to me that they were doing it on their own, without any guidance from HR officials, who understood federal personnel procedures.

That afternoon, I called a virtual meeting for all remaining GH staff. I knew from Ramona's experience the previous week to be wary of such meetings, that they might be recorded and leaked, and so I should be vigilant about what I said. But I didn't care about any of that. I just wanted to get the few remaining people together, in case they were feeling as lonely as I was. As the call started, I realized how little information I had to share. I told them that I imagined they might be feeling alone and scared. I told them I was scared, too—scared for myself, scared for our colleagues, and scared about the future.

"I don't know what's coming next," I said. "But I'm trying to get answers, and in the interim I wanted to provide some space for us to connect for a few minutes. I wanted to thank those of you who reached out over the past twenty-four hours offering to help. I'm sorry that I haven't responded to so many of you, but please know that your kind words and generosity have not gone unnoticed. The truth is, at this point I just don't know what you can do to help; I don't even know how I can help."

I didn't want to end on that sad note, but I had no other note to end on. So I promised to keep them informed as soon as I had anything to share and wrapped up the call, feeling as helpless as I had all day.

At nine thirty that evening, an unsigned message from "Internal Communications" was sent out agency-wide, under the subject line "The Path Forward." It stated that all remaining staff would be placed on administrative leave by the end of the week, except for "essential personnel," who would be designated by Thursday, February 6.

The email made reference to plans to return all overseas USAID personnel to the U.S. within thirty days, a time frame that would force American foreign service officers to pull their children out of schools midsemester, cancel emergency medical procedures, and pack up their lives and families while they were also responsible for managing USAID's programs in each country. The message concluded, blandly, "Thank you for your service."

On Wednesday, Nida, Ramona, and I went to the Reagan Building to finally meet with Joel Borkert and the USAID leadership team. We made our way through the eerily empty headquarters building and entered the administrator's suite, where we were ushered into the executive conference room. I had last been there years earlier, during the first Trump administration, to brief Administrator Mark Green on our proposed restructuring of our tuberculosis strategy. I remembered nervously trying to answer pointed questions from Green and several of his top deputies, who had relentlessly pushed us to identify opportunities to make our programs more efficient, to maximize local ownership, and to propel host governments toward self-reliance, reducing the need for foreign assistance from the United States.

Today, the room felt emptier, devoid of the expertise and experience that had so often directed policy from within its walls. Besides the three of us from GH, the group consisted of Joel Borkert (USAID's chief of staff), Adam Korzeniewski (White House liaison), Meghan Hanson (director of policy), Paul Seong (senior advisor to the administrator), and Ken Jackson (with Pete Marocco's new designation as deputy administrator, Ken's title was revised to acting deputy administrator for management and resources). Jason Gray (briefly the acting administrator, now back to chief information officer) joined as well. The group looked tired and bored, and I got the sense that we were not the first bureau to brief this group on our "mission-critical functions" that afternoon.

Without introductions, Joel, who was eating a frozen Indian dinner, jumped right in. "In full transparency, we're drawing down USAID," he said. "We'd like you to walk us through your mission-critical functions so that we can close things out smoothly. What are the key priorities that we need to keep working on in GH, and the staff needs to carry them out?"

Draw down. Close out. The words he dropped so casually rang in my head. Our global health programs didn't concern him, he was only interested in the quickest way to shutter the agency. I knew this was my only chance to make him see why our work mattered.

"Thanks, Joel," I began. "With the current pause on foreign aid, we're primarily focused right now on the waiver to restart our lifesaving activities. But emergency response is only a tiny fraction of our work. So much of what we do is to strengthen sustainable health systems around the world for long-term health improvements. Let me tell you about that work as well as some of the more urgent needs."

Joel, who had been checking his watch, shrugged and took another bite of his microwaved paneer. Just as I was about to go on, Paul Seong spoke up. "I'd say just stick to the lifesaving stuff," he said. Aside from Jason Gray, Paul was the only career official representing the front office in this meeting. My only prior engagement with Paul was the Ebola briefing on Monday after which he had asked for the names of the meeting's participants, who had been the only staff spared from administrative leave that day. Paul had been a relatively junior foreign service officer until recently, when he had somehow ingratiated himself with our new political leaders. Now the political appointees seemed to look to him for strategic advice on how to tear down the agency, and he appeared to relish his newfound influence, which was affirmed by his seat at the center of the conference table. Joel and the others nodded their agreement.

Disappointed, though not surprised, I began to describe various lifesaving components of USAID's global health portfolio, highlighting how we prepare for and respond to emerging pandemic threats; support the diagnosis and treatment of tuberculosis, malaria, and HIV; and immunize millions of children from the deadliest childhood diseases. I spoke for about five minutes, focusing primarily on our infectious diseases work and hoping to keep the attention of people who seemed to have no experience—or interest—in global health.

When I finished, the room was silent, the political appointees looking at one another in what appeared to be disbelief. The silence was broken by Ken Jackson, who chuckled softly and shook his head. "Wow, there really is so much that USAID does that we never knew," he said. "This is the story that needs to get out there."

Joel, also smiling, chimed in next, echoing Jackson's amazement. "I had no idea you did all this," he said. "As a Republican, when I think of what USAID does in global health, I assumed it was just, you know, abortions."

I didn't know whether to laugh or cry. My first thought was to explain that no global health programming supports abortions. Providing or promoting abortions with foreign assistance funds is illegal, and we had robust systems in place to ensure that no U.S. funds were used to support abortions. But obviously, arguing with Joel would get me nowhere. Mostly, I was shocked to hear how unapologetically ignorant our new leaders were about USAID's work. Just the night before, they had triumphantly announced that nearly the entire agency was being placed on administrative leave, clearly without having a clue as to what we did. I willed myself to avoid eye contact with Nida or Ramona, knowing that seeing their expressions would lay waste to my twitching attempt at a straight face.

The first question came from Adam Korzeniewski, a veteran of the first Trump administration where he served short stints with the departments of Treasury and Commerce. Adam, the White House liaison to USAID, wanted to know more about the risks associated with interruptions to TB clinical trials, which I had mentioned in my overview. He was the only participant in this meeting who appeared genuinely happy to be there, and he was wearing a USAID lapel pin on his suit jacket, in what I could only explain as an apparently ironic nod to the agency he was charged with destroying. I found it odd and vaguely offensive, like a vindictive landlord throwing a farewell party for a tenant he was in the process of evicting.

"Some of the studies are testing new treatment regimens for drug-resistant tuberculosis," I explained, hoping I could convey the very real danger in terms that would register with this audience. "Thousands of enrolled patients are at risk now that their lifesaving treatment is stopped. But that's not the only danger. We only have limited options to treat drug-resistant TB. We're using our antibiotics of last resort in these trials. Interrupting treatment midstream risks the development of new, even more drug-resistant strains that could be untreatable. For an airborne infectious disease, that is a serious national security risk."

Adam thought for a moment and then responded, noting that the political appointees at USAID were "not health people." It would be hard, he surmised, for nonexperts to understand this issue. And so he suggested that we draft a simple, "Barney-style" set of slides to help the political leadership grasp the dangers, referring to the purple dinosaur of children's television. He recommended that we use the term "Super TB" instead of "drug-resistant TB" to describe the mutations that can develop when treatment is interrupted, because it might be more likely to "catch their attention."

Adam then made clear that he did not count himself among those political appointees who were not health experts. Though he had no relevant training or experience, he reassured me that he understood the severity of infectious diseases, noting that he had recently read a book about smallpox. Apparently he had watched movies as well.

"One thing I thought of while you were talking," he added, gesticulating wildly with his hands to conjure the image in his mind. "If you can make one of those maps like they have in *Outbreak*, where it shows the red growing over time as the disease spreads? You know, like the zombie apocalypse? That would be great, very effective."

The thought that Adam might have the most health expertise of anyone in the agency's leadership made me shudder.

Meghan Hanson, who had been appointed days ago as USAID's new director of policy, focused on my warnings related to the interruption of activities needed to prevent the spread of malaria, one of the world's leading killers of children. I had noted that the rainy season was fast approaching in many of the African countries with the highest burden of malaria, and that the annual preparations to combat the disease—indoor residual spraying, distribution of bed nets, delivery of commodities for testing and treatment—had all been stopped.

Hanson seemed to grasp the urgency. "We need to get those activities turned back on right away," she said. "Write up the details, including the number of lives at risk, how quickly the interventions are needed, and where, and get that to us tonight!"

I told her that we would prioritize this action. But, I reminded her, all the malaria division staff—the entirety of USAID's malaria expertise—had been shut off from USAID's network, making it extremely difficult to pull together accurate information quickly.

At this, Joel's exasperation with DOGE's meddling boiled over, and he shouted at the room: "See, this is why, just because it might work at Twitter does not mean you can do it here!"

I shifted uncomfortably in my chair. If the political appointees in this room—tearing down USAID without any comprehension of the consequences—felt that *DOGE's* tactics were reckless and destructive, we were in deeper trouble than I had realized.

Following another long silence, Joel summarized what we needed to do next. My description of our lifesaving work had been helpful, and we would need to develop "a very simple way to describe it to the secretary," he told us. "To be clear, we're not looking for a laundry list of everything you want to do, you're going to have to cut things, it's going to have to be draconian. You're only going to get things that are priority number one, that is all we're going to be able to do, so don't even send up the things that are priorities number two, three, or four."

At that point, Nida jumped in. Out of the corner of my eye, I had noticed her picking nervously at her hands for most of the meeting, and I knew it was just a matter of time before my oft-impatient colleague spoke up.

"Can I just clarify one thing?" she asked, not waiting for a response. "This group seems very focused on what GH does to respond to infectious diseases, but we haven't spoken much about our other lifesaving work. Just as one example, we support lifesaving care to mothers for emergency interventions like postpartum hemorrhaging and eclampsia, two of the leading causes of pregnancy-related deaths. You would also consider that kind of work to fit into our 'priority number one,' right?"

Another brief silence followed as Joel watched the clock, and it was Paul Seong who broke it. "I'd say that's more of a number two," he said dismissively, looking to Joel and Ken for affirmation.

"That sounds right," Joel agreed, and the others nodded. Nida, shaking visibly, scribbled furiously in her notebook. And just like that, it was decided. Without even a cursory nod to data or expertise, USAID's leadership had determined purely on a whim that lifesaving maternal health services were not a priority for this administration.

Finally, Joel told us where things now stood. "As I said, the decision has been made to draw down USAID," he said. "My job is to make sure it goes smoothly, and I need your help with that. I need you to tell me which individuals you need to do those few core remaining activities. It's gotta be lean, but if you need us to bring a few people back to life—turn them back on—we can do that. Everyone else is going to stay off." He glanced at Jason Gray, who apparently was in charge of turning people on and off. Jason nodded, almost imperceptibly, without looking up.

As the meeting ended, I reminded Joel that we were still waiting on his approval of our approach to implement the waiver for lifesaving activities, and that we had also sent him several requests to initiate our increasingly delayed response to the Ebola outbreak in Uganda. Then we were ushered out to the elevator.

Ramona, Nida, and I sat in the food court in the basement of the Reagan Building, trying to process the meeting we had just left. It was simply shocking that the group currently sitting in the administrator's suite was the team that was making decisions about USAID's future. They were not real policymakers, but impostors, sitting in big chairs and pretending to grapple with complex issues that required teams of experts, who they had just off-loaded. Clearly, they hadn't considered how their plans to dismantle USAID might affect lives around the world or the health and safety of Americans. Now, having heard my warnings, they were not actually interested in— or capable of—finding a solution to prevent people from dying.

Their job was to tear down the agency as quickly and quietly as possible, receive their pat on the back from Pete Marocco, and move on to whatever was next.

Ramona, Nida, and I had been dismissed from the meeting with an impossible assignment: to provide a "draconian" short list of global health activities to maintain during the "drawdown" and a rank-ordered list of the staff needed to accomplish them. We did not know where to start. Were we really supposed to just abandon all of USAID's programs to strengthen health systems, even though they were the key to our sustainable development goals? Had they really just deprioritized our maternal and child health programs in front of our eyes? And how could we even begin to rank our staff?

Ramona summed things up: "They're asking us to dig our own grave."

That evening, I called Atul Gawande. I had not spoken to him since his resignation two and a half weeks earlier, but he did not sound surprised to hear my voice. I tried my best to describe the past couple of weeks, how unprepared I felt to lead GH during this period of mayhem, and how I was overwhelmed by the constant barrage of destruction of our staff, our work, and our agency. I also mentioned the growing pit in my stomach about the Ebola outbreak, where we were making no inroads. I didn't know what I wanted from him. Advice? Reassurance? Just to let him know what was happening to the organization he had so recently led?

Atul was calming and supportive. He told me that he felt terrible that I was in this impossible position, and he offered me advice on how to prioritize. He encouraged me to stay focused on implementing Rubio's waiver, which was the one area where we might be able to make an impact right now. He advised me to not agree to do anything illegal and reminded me that part of my job was to ensure that the political leadership understood the consequences of their decisions, so I ought to put my concerns in writing. He offered to make some calls to find out where things stood on

Ebola, and to see if he could convince people he knew at other agencies or nongovernmental organizations to help pick up USAID's slack.

Finally, he told me that my most important job might not be related to global health at all. "You're in a unique position to witness this destruction, Nick," he said. "If all else fails, your job is to bear witness."

12

An Irrational Equation (Day 18)

Thursday, February 6, started out with some good news. At 2:53 a.m., Joel Borkert approved our memo authorizing GH to restart lifesaving activities. By sunrise, Ramona and Nida had already compiled a list of projects that I was now authorized to approve. Allowable activities included delivery of health services, emergency response to infectious disease outbreaks, supply chain management, and essential medicines, testing supplies, and other commodities. Although we had proposed a ninety-day timeline to match the length of the foreign assistance pause, Joel's order required us to limit the definition only to include activities that were needed to avert loss of human life within the next thirty days.

Only being able to consider a one-month horizon for whether an activity was needed to save lives was, of course, antithetical to sound public health policy. It meant that many key activities would be arbitrarily excluded. To take just one example, it would exclude placing orders for new drugs and commodities that, while not needed within thirty days, had significant lag time between when an order was placed and when it was received. Because we couldn't make orders that extended beyond thirty days, we were creating an inevitable backlog. Similarly, the shortened time frame prevented us from restarting critical outbreak prevention activities because the lives that would be saved fell outside the one-month window. Still, the approved memo was a win, as we could finally restart several critical activities that were needed to save lives right away.

Unfortunately, I was in no position to celebrate this small victory. My morning was subsumed by the chaotic scramble to identify who would be included in the small number of "essential staff" who would be spared from administrative leave to maintain the agency's few remaining critical functions as USAID was closed down. The agency notice from Tuesday ("The Path Forward") had specified that all essential staff would be notified by 3 p.m. on Thursday, yet, by that morning, we still didn't even know GH's target number.

Finally, around 10 a.m., Joel informed bureau leaders that of the more than ten thousand USAID staff working in more than one hundred countries, the agency could retain only 611 as "essential personnel" worldwide. He said that each bureau would soon be allocated a specific number of positions to maintain and would have a brief window to send names and emails for the staff we chose to prioritize. He had no guidance or expectations on how to select these staff members, telling us, "How you determine the names is up to you."

At 10:45 a.m., Joel emailed me GH's allocation: "The denominator for GH is 132." His misuse of the term *denominator* made the math no less stark; 132 was actually the numerator in an irrational equation: We could keep only 132 of the 783 individuals who worked in GH on January 20.

The previous evening, working with Nida, Ramona, and Natalia, I had drafted a list of nearly one hundred staff who would need to be retained to carry out our primary functions, which had been limited to implementing the lifesaving humanitarian assistance waiver. It had been a disheartening and painful process. There was no objective way to rank our colleagues against one another, so we instead focused on the functions that we knew were needed, and those that we would have to deprioritize given our pared-down scope. Still, the list was insufficient, and it was clear that critical needs would go unfulfilled.

Without parameters, we didn't even know what our options were. Could we include our bureau leaders, like Julie Wallace, who had been on administrative leave for nearly two weeks, or were they off-limits due to the circumstances of their removal? Certainly we needed them. I thought we could put them on our list. I had serious doubts that the administration was still interested in investigating the fifty-eight senior officials. DOGE had already accomplished its goal of sowing chaos throughout the agency by removing them temporarily.

No one would even notice, I argued. The front office was only interested in the final number, they didn't care about the names. As I had suspected with my ninth-grade social studies teacher, they probably wouldn't even read our list. "I bet we could put Hillary Clinton's name on there, and they would approve it," I joked. Natalia and Nida thought we should keep our leaders off the list, given that they had been specifically identified for discipline. Eventually, we compromised on including just one of our four deputy assistant administrators on our essential staff list, reasoning that this person had been serving in the leadership role only in an acting capacity. (Sure enough, the administration never noticed or cared that we planned to bring back one of the career officials they had targeted for removal.)

As difficult as this exercise would have been under any conditions, it was made nearly impossible by the fact that our numbers continued to be cut throughout the day. Less than an hour after giving us our target number for GH of 132, Joel called a virtual meeting for all bureau heads and informed us that Pete Marocco had just directed that we needed to make further cuts. The 611 number was out; now USAID could retain only 297 people in total. Joel promised to provide updated bureau-specific numbers shortly, noting that our lists still needed to be finalized right away. One of the other bureau heads came off mute and told Joel that it was not realistic to make any further cuts without jeopardizing lives around the world. Joel responded that there was no room to negotiate the levels. We needed to provide the list of names at the lower number. If we had concerns, we could discuss those afterward.

At 12:06 p.m., Joel emailed to inform me that GH's "final number" was seventy-seven, noting that Paul Seong would follow up soon with more details.

At 12:20, Paul emailed me with a new number for GH: Now we were down to forty-four.

At 12:26, Joel wrote: "I need this in 15 minutes, otherwise, your people will not be on the list. Names and emails are all I need."

The insanity of the exercise was matched by the irrationality of the numbers being tossed around. Our list, insufficient as it was, relied on the assumptions that USAID staff would remain at overseas missions to implement health programs and that the operational support staff needed to implement our programs (legal, contracting, financial, IT, HR, etc.), housed at USAID but outside of GH, would continue. Now we learned that those assumptions were wrong. The regional bureaus, which we had assumed would include sufficient staffing in each country to implement our health programs, were especially decimated. The latest list proposed, for example, that only twelve staffers would be retained for the entire continent of Africa, and only eight for Asia, not even one person per country. Furthermore, there was no allocation at all for critical functions like legal or human resources.

The leaders of several regional bureaus reached out to me in rapid succession, pleading with me to allocate some of GH's slots to them. Tensions were high. The ever-dwindling numbers did not just represent the organizational structure needed to make our programs work—we were talking about people, who would stay and who would go. While I agreed that there was no way USAID would be able to implement health programs in countries without sufficient staffing in those missions, I did not have extra positions to spare within GH. Besides, horse-trading among the bureaus was futile; there simply were not enough positions to go around. I quickly called an emergency meeting with all the regional bureaus, hoping we could align on what to do.

In the meeting, we all agreed that the proposed numbers were not feasible, even to safely close out the agency, much less to restart and continue lifesaving programs. But this was the directive we had received from our political leadership, so what option did we have? I argued that there was no point in providing a list at the levels we were being allocated.

"Staffing at these levels will result in total failure," I said. "If we give them lists of staff at those levels, then we will end up being blamed when everything collapses. They'll say, 'The career officials told us the staff they needed and we gave it to them, so it's their fault that things didn't work.'"

Instead, I proposed that we simply provide a list of the minimum staff required for each of our bureaus to carry out the identified functions. "If the front office wants to cut further, that's on them," I said. "But we should not do their dirty work for them. I don't want to be seen as endorsing a list that we know won't work."

My proposal was met with mixed reactions. Brian Frantz, who ran the Bureau for Africa, seemed to agree with my approach, but cautioned that, if it backfired, we would lose control over which staff we absolutely needed to keep. Others argued that it was our job to carry out the task that was assigned; this was a political decision, and our job was to help the political leadership achieve its goals. To refuse the assignment was insubordination. The result would be our removal, and then someone else would end up making the list they wanted.

Unfortunately, according to Joel's latest email, we were out of time to debate, and we had to make a decision. I told the group that the list I planned to submit for GH would be the minimum level necessary to perform our core functions, but it would not be as low as the forty-four we were most recently allocated. I implored them to do the same, given that GH's programs could not survive without sufficient staffing at our missions. I thought I saw several nods as the call ended, but clearly I misread the group.

In the end, I submitted a list of seventy-seven staff for GH, which I considered the bare minimum—honestly, far below the bare minimum—that would be needed to carry out lifesaving activities and close out the remaining health programs, and even this was dependent on there being sufficient mission and operational staffing. But all the regional bureaus submitted lists at the outrageously minuscule levels in Paul Seong's final spreadsheet: twelve for Africa, eight for Asia, twenty-one for the Middle East, ten for Europe and Eurasia, eight for Latin America and the Caribbean. At these levels, our programs had no chance of success. Regret set in immediately.

Nida, Ramona, and I decided that we needed to share our concerns for the record, even if it was unlikely to make any difference.

That evening, the three of us gathered at my house, eating pizza and drafting an email to Joel. Though we all agreed that we needed to register our dissent, we had different goals for the message, and we spent more than an hour ironing out our differences.

Ramona was apoplectic and ready for the email to serve as her letter of resignation. "At some point, we become complicit," she said. "I cannot keep helping them dismantle our agency."

Nida was on the other end of the spectrum, believing we still could make a difference from within, and so she kept editing out Ramona's proposed sign-off—"it has been the honor of a lifetime . . ."—from the draft email. "It's not time to give up yet," she argued. "We still might be able to restart some activities under the waiver. We can't stop trying. Plus, there is no way what they're doing is legal. Maybe Congress or the courts will step in." The language Ramona was proposing was too inflammatory, Nida thought. Even if we didn't resign, the email would probably get us fired, and we needed to tone it down a bit.

I fell somewhere in the middle, still haunted by Ramona's observation the previous day that our role had been reduced to grave digging. But resigning was a scary prospect. Even if I didn't like the looks of the road ahead for USAID, I was afraid to give up the job I had loved all these years. The deal-breaker for me was the staff who remained at GH. Whether I deserved it or not, I was the leader of GH, and I felt that to resign now would be to abandon them in the middle of a crisis.

Eventually, we reached a compromise. The language needed to be strong, but not incendiary, and though we wouldn't proactively resign, if the email got us fired, we would be okay with that. Jordanna, who had been listening to us argue all this time from the kitchen, was our final reviewer. With an eye toward not getting us fired, she removed the phrase "FULL STOP" and several other unnecessary flourishes. The final version, which I sent (under all our names) at 9:34 p.m. to Joel Borkert, Ken Jackson, Paul Seong, and Jason Gray, with copies to all the regional bureau heads, stated:

> We must express in the strongest possible terms that the directive to create a rank-ordered list of . . . personnel globally is deeply concerning and dangerous, as it directly undermines the safety and well-being of both American citizens and vulnerable populations worldwide who rely on USAID's lifesaving global health programming. . . .
>
> GH's minimal remaining staffing list . . . even in its current form, will put millions of lives at risk in the short term, as well as compromise our ability to be responsible stewards of U.S. taxpayer resources.
>
> The greatest risk, however, is the absence of Mission-based staff. Without adequate Mission presence, including USAID Health Officers, implementation of lifesaving assistance and effective outbreak response cannot occur.
>
> Reducing the USAID global health workforce in Washington and at Missions to such minimal levels is tantamount to condemning lives. As you know, there is an escalating Ebola outbreak in Uganda right now. Insufficient staffing to address this crisis directly jeopardizes the safety of American citizens. We have a moral obligation to avoid that outcome at all costs.
>
> We urge you to reconsider any attempt to pursue this course of action in order to avoid these devastating consequences. The lives of millions depend on decisions made with care, consideration, and a commitment to humanity.

With the email sent, Ramona and Nida headed home, and we braced ourselves for the response to the most strongly worded objection any of us had ever sent to our agency's leadership. But there was no blowback. They never even responded.

13.

Approved for Termination (Days 19–21)

On Friday morning, February 7, I was once again summoned to the Ronald Reagan Building. Meghan Hanson, USAID's newly appointed director of policy, emailed me and some of my colleagues from the Bureau for Humanitarian Assistance to urgently join the inaugural meeting of something she called the "Programs Group."

"We need to meet at the RRB shortly," Hanson wrote. "Is everyone in the building?" Meghan somehow seemed unaware that the agency had closed its headquarters facilities earlier in the week and that all USAID employees had been directed to stay home. After my experiences so far that week, I did not want to participate in any high-level meeting on my own, so I asked Alyssa Jernigan, GH's budget director, to join me. The only complication was that the meeting was supposed to start in just forty minutes. I hopped on my bike and booked it downtown, where I met Alyssa, who had thrown on a professional outfit and jumped in a cab. Then we entered the building that until recently bore the insignia of USAID. We rode the elevator in silence to the sixth floor, wondering what would be in store for us that day.

Entering the administrator's suite, the disarray was immediately apparent, with people scuttling in and out of view in all directions. On the way in, we bumped into a gray-haired man sporting a boxy suit and an impatient grimace. "Finally," he said without introducing himself. "Are you the ones who're going to tell us what we're doing here today?" Alyssa and I briefly exchanged a look, instant confirmation that neither of us knew who we were talking to, or what he was talking about.

Before I could attempt a response, Adam Korzeniewski, the White House liaison who had suggested "Barney-style" slides the last time we met, walked into the anteroom with Jason Gray. "Welcome, welcome, I see you've met Tim," Adam said with a flourish. Once again he was wearing a USAID pin on his lapel, and it continued to irk me. Tim, it turned out, was Timothy Meisburger, the political appointee assigned to lead USAID's Bureau for Humanitarian Assistance.

"Nice to meet you, Tim," I said. "Hopefully someone else knows the plan. Alyssa and I are at least as lost as you are." Tim rolled his eyes.

"Thanks for coming upstairs. Remind me, which floor do you work on again?" Adam asked. Baffled, I wondered: Does no one in the USAID front office remember that they barred the staff from coming to work? Leaving aside the fact that GH had been located in a different building for years, did anyone here even realize that the building was completely empty except for them?

Instead of answering, I turned to Jason, and asked hopefully if, by chance, he knew why we had been assembled that morning. "Don't look at me," he said with a sad chuckle. His eyes dropped to his feet. "I'm just the stuckee around here." (I had never heard the term, so I looked it up later. Urban Dictionary defines a stuckee as "the only person in an organization that can operate a piece of equipment or software, thus becoming stuck with it forever.")

So we waited around awkwardly until Meghan Hanson arrived. Both Tim and Meghan seemed unsure of where to hold the meeting, as if there weren't dozens of empty conference rooms available. Meghan suggested that there might be meeting space in a "dasha" conference room, if anyone knew where that was. I didn't remember there being any conference rooms with Russian names in the RRB, but Alyssa realized she was referring to the defunct acronym "DCHA"—the Bureau for Democracy, Conflict, and Humanitarian Assistance, an operating unit that had not existed since an agency reorganization during the first Trump administration.

Alyssa and I knew the space Meghan was referring to (though mispronouncing), having both worked in the building earlier in our careers, and led the group to the conference room. Along the way, Meghan asked, "Do your badges work in here?"

Sounding insulted, Alyssa snapped, "Yes, they do." She told me later that she felt as if we were being treated like guests in our own home by intruders who didn't even know where the bathroom was.

When we got to the conference room, Meghan explained why she had convened us. Overnight, the political leadership at the State Department and USAID had established a new "Coordination Support Team" to manage the logistical challenges of dismantling USAID. In its first meeting, the CST had discussed the various glitches that were arising and attempted to group them into several workstreams: personnel, IT, finances, contracts, facilities, and security, among others. For each workstream, a subgroup would be responsible for resolving challenges within its purview.

Meghan recounted, without a hint of satire, how toward the end of the CST meeting, one additional workstream was identified as an afterthought. "Someone said they had seen something on the news about emergency food supplies rotting in a warehouse somewhere," she recalled. "And then someone else said, 'And what about global health?' We sort of realized that if that was happening to food in warehouses it could be happening to medicine and stuff, too. So now we're setting up another working group to deal with challenges related to programs. Since that includes both humanitarian assistance and global health, we wanted both your bureaus to be in the Programs Group to resolve any program-related issues that may come up during the drawdown. Are there any questions?"

I had more questions now than I did when I was standing dumbly in the administrator's suite.

Our small group in that room was supposed to resolve "any program-related issues" when all our work around the world had been abruptly frozen for nearly three weeks and the staff who manage that work was being slashed? It was like asking us to figure out why a plane wouldn't fly after removing the engine. But if this was our only opportunity to influence USAID's political leadership to restart our most critical lifesaving programs, we needed to take it seriously. Alyssa, ever the pragmatist, was way ahead of me. She jumped right in, ticking off the problems to be addressed: Stop-work orders needed to be rescinded for contracts to restart lifesaving activities; the external communications ban needed to be at least partially lifted to enable effective coordination for activities that were continuing or ending; payments to partners needed to be processed so they could resume their work; staffing for essential programs needed to be reinstated in Washington and overseas—

"Wait!" Tim interrupted her, jumping to his feet. I thought he was going to make a suggestion to help us triage the challenges we faced. But his interjection was of a more mundane nature: "We have a flip chart here, but no markers. We need markers!"

Markers, of course, were not what we needed. What we needed, if we were going to avoid catastrophic consequences, was a reprieve from the haphazard hacking apart of our agency. I told Meghan and Tim as much, but they just shook their heads.

"That's not gonna happen," Tim said, rolling his eyes as if I had told him what we needed was a time machine. "You need to come to terms with the fact that USAID is dead. We're just trying to mitigate the damage that's done on our way out."

Meghan was not much more optimistic, though her tone was less dismissive. This was now the second time I had met her, and in both meetings I got the sense that she had been looking forward to directing actual policy at USAID, not presiding over the agency's chaotic destruction. "Why don't you write up what you think you need and send it to me? Like Tim said, I don't think we're going to reverse course, but at least we'll have your recommendations."

I replied that Alyssa and I would work on drafting something, recognizing that at least we would have another opportunity to put our warnings on the record. Committed to his approach of flip-charting our way out of this mess, Tim left the room in search of a pack of markers. As the rest of us stood up to leave, Meghan asked Alyssa and me to stay in the building so we could reconvene later if needed. She noted that there were plenty of empty cubicles available for us to squat in.

Walking through the dark, quiet floor was like visiting the ruins of Pompeii; the eerie, postapocalyptic feel of daily routine frozen in time. Workspaces were adorned with bright artwork and happy photos. Paperwork in progress was splayed across desktops. Decorative bowls brimmed with candy intended for passersby. Extra pairs of work pumps were tucked neatly under desks, ready to be swapped out for commuting sneakers. These were the abandoned cubicles of our colleagues; many had sat at them for years, and then left one day like they did every other, expecting to return the next morning. Only this time, no one had come back.

Alyssa and I set up shop in the largest corner office we could find—why not?—and connected our laptops to begin drafting our recommendations for the Programs Group. But as soon as I was online, my inbox alerted me to a new crisis: DOGE had ordered the immediate termination of approximately eight hundred USAID contracts. A handful of these contracts (which we called "awards") were managed by GH, and the agency's contracting officers were asking our GH project managers to assess whether it was okay for the awards to be terminated. Aside from the fact that most of the project managers were on administrative leave, and thus unreachable, it was unclear how they could make an assessment even if they were still working. Somehow, the list of the condemned contracts had made its way to Nida, who now flagged it for me.

I did not think it was okay for the contracts to be terminated. I did not understand on what grounds they were being terminated, and I assumed there were legal implications for terminating contracts without cause. I didn't want to create even a perception that GH project managers were authorizing contracting officers to terminate these awards, so I asked Jami Rodgers and Nadeem Shah, who led USAID's contracting office, to make sure any requests to terminate GH contracts went directly to me.

But the question of whether it was legal for DOGE to order the termination of USAID contracts was not my primary concern. The bigger issue was that terminating our contracts represented an alarming escalation in DOGE's efforts to dismantle the agency. Up to this point, we understood that our programs were to be paused for ninety days while the administration conducted a review, which gave us an opportunity to justify the value of our work and identify the mission-critical programs that needed to continue. Terminating contracts now, without conducting any review, no longer sounded like a temporary pause—this would have permanent consequences. Furthermore, Rubio had issued a waiver to the pause for lifesaving activities. Even if USAID was being closed down, the secretary of state had committed to continuing this limited set of critical programs. How could we comply with the waiver and resume our lifesaving work if the contracts needed to implement those activities were terminated? I told Jami and Nadeem that GH would need to review any contracts slated for termination in advance, to at least ensure that they were not needed to implement lifesaving activities.

Nadeem agreed to let GH review the awards quickly, but he explained that his office was under extreme time pressure to execute the terminations. He was required to provide updates to Jeremy Lewin, the DOGE team leader, at 3 p.m., 5 p.m., and 7 p.m. to report his team's progress on how many terminations had been finalized. Also, he had been told that the contracts had already been reviewed for applicable waivers or exceptions, and none of them applied. I asked Nadeem who had conducted those reviews, and what information sources they were based on, but he did not know. I could not think of any way that such reviews could have been conducted without consulting with the project managers, who were familiar with the contracts, which had not happened. I thanked him for giving us a brief window to double-check and promised that we would work quickly.

My team reviewed each of the dozen or so GH contracts on the list, seeking to identify if any of the activities fit into the lifesaving category. We found that at least one contract that provided medicine for several tropical diseases in West Africa was on the list to be terminated. I immediately notified Jami and Nadeem, recommending that it not be terminated because it was covered under Rubio's waiver. They thanked me for catching it and said they would try to hold off on the termination. The other contracts did not appear to meet the definition of "lifesaving activities" and were terminated that day. Even so, several of them were critically important, including contracts to conduct surveillance and collect data on infectious diseases, to train healthcare workers on safe childbirth procedures and infection control, and to keep governments informed of when they were running low on drug supplies and needed to order more. It pained me to let these efforts lapse, but I felt I had no choice.

It was clear to me that we were fighting a losing battle. Our programs were being terminated—not just paused—and our staff was being fired or shunted to administrative leave. Still we could not give up. So at four o'clock that afternoon, I sent the response that Meghan had requested, noting that it was "by no means comprehensive but at least would get us into a position to start trying to effectively restart lifesaving humanitarian assistance."

In order to implement lifesaving humanitarian health assistance and avoid unnecessary death, USAID GH needs the following:

- Restored access and pause on administrative leave notices for at least 6 weeks for all relevant mission staff needed to implement lifesaving health programs, including, but not limited to Contracting, Regional Legal, Executive, Health, and Humanitarian Officers globally, who are responsible for the oversight and implementation of ~85% of global health funding which is programmed [in countries].
- Complete access restored and administrative leave notices revoked for relevant Washington-based GH offices . . .
- Access to the full breadth of GH-specific programmatic and operational support within and beyond the GH Bureau at HQ including, but not limited to, General Counsel, Contracting Officers, IT, and CFO for at least 6 weeks.

- Pause on any global health-focused award terminations until a determination is made as to whether the mechanisms are needed to implement lifesaving humanitarian assistance.
- Blanket resumption of payment services for all health and humanitarian partners/projects carrying out critical lifesaving assistance so that they can be paid for work conducted prior to the pause on foreign assistance as well as for the lifesaving activities currently permitted under the Waiver.

Failure to do the above will result in not only the risk of immediate loss of life, but risk further deaths and escalating spread of deadly disease, including to the U.S.

I wasn't holding my breath that it would work, but it felt good, at least, to put it in writing.

That night, for the first time that long week, we finally got some good news. Only hours before the midnight deadline, a federal district judge issued a temporary restraining order preventing the administration from placing the vast majority of USAID's staff on administrative leave. The order required that everyone who had already been placed on leave be returned to regular work status and reconnected to their email and other USAID systems. The reprieve was only temporary, of course, but it was the first sign that anyone in a position to do something about the dismantling of our agency was paying attention.

I imagine that Joel Borkert, Ken Jackson, Meghan Hanson, and the others who were tasked with orchestrating the orderly "drawdown" of USAID were nearly as relieved by the court's ruling as I was. They had no plan in place and were just starting to realize the complexity of the agency they were trying to undo. Based on the warnings they had received from me and from the other career officials, they were well aware that if USAID's staff had been slashed to just three hundred people that night, the results would have been a colossal disaster.

For me, the court's order was a much-needed chance for a reset. Many of our staff would be returning from administrative leave on Monday (although, sadly, none of the 374 contractor staff who had been terminated), and that influx would allow us to focus on restarting lifesaving activities, rather than bouncing from one manufactured crisis to the next. Most important, our leadership team would be coming back, including my supervisor, Julie Wallace. I hoped this would inject a dose of normalcy into what had become a daily routine of chaos. Even though Julie and the other GH leaders had been on administrative leave for only two weeks, they had missed so much. I didn't think it could wait until Monday, so I arranged for a Sunday morning meeting to bring everyone up to speed.

And so, on the morning of Sunday, February 9, Ramona, Nida, and I met with Julie and two of her deputies, Carmen Coles and Han Kang, at an apartment building across the street from the USAID Annex in L'Enfant Plaza. Incredibly, out the window we could see the USAID flag still flying atop our former office building, whipping back and forth in the blustery wind. While the demolition teams had removed all street-level signage, they had missed the rooftop flag emblazoned with USAID's insignia, a final, defiant vestige that proved the continued existence of our agency, despite DOGE's best efforts to erase us.

The meeting started awkwardly. I brought coffee. Someone else had picked up pastries. Ramona, a Swiftie at heart, had made friendship bracelets for everyone, beaded with cute messages like USAID4EVA. Despite the pleasantries, however, I was nervous to revisit what had happened over the past two weeks. With all our work frozen, our buildings closed, and most of our staff gone, certainly no one could summarize my tenure as acting assistant administrator as an overwhelming success.

The last time this group met, we would have been discussing normal business, from which we all now seemed so far removed. No one knew where to start. Han, the deputy assistant administrator overseeing our HIV work, was the top-ranking foreign service officer at GH. He had a knack for always knowing obscure holidays and national observance days. Now, as he poured himself a coffee, he tried to break the ice by announcing that International Café au Lait Day was coming up the following week. Then we all made small talk—*There's a day for everything! They should give out free coffees that day!*—until Nida abruptly cut us off.

"What are we doing?" she asked. "Our entire agency is imploding. Why are we talking about International Coffee Day right now? Shouldn't we be talking about how we're going to stop this?"

That got us on track. I took a deep breath and began recounting the events of the past two weeks, with Nida and Ramona filling in details I missed. I described the political appointees and their tenuous grasp of what USAID does. I described how DOGE had cut off email access, closed buildings, and removed our signage and hallway art. I tried to convey the fear and confusion among the remaining staff and our ongoing struggles to make any progress. We finally had an approved process to restart lifesaving activities, but no activities were actually restarting because we were unable to move any funds. Neither DOGE nor the political appointees had shown any interest; their only goal was to close the agency as quickly and quietly as possible. USAID's new political leaders had made it clear that our job was to dig our own grave, and we had been directed to take actions that were improper and possibly illegal, like agreeing to the termination of our contracts and ranking our staff to be slashed. We had made lists of essential personnel, and even though we had registered our warnings that the planned cuts would cripple our ability to operate and would cost lives around the world, those warnings had gone unheeded. If not for the eleventh-hour judicial intervention, the cuts would have gone into effect. One key takeaway, for me, was that I would never again agree to make lists of staff that would be used to demolish the ability of our bureau to function.

Then I addressed the elephant in the room. "Hopefully this goes without saying, but I want to say it anyway," I said. "My designation as acting assistant administrator was the result of illegitimate action by DOGE to remove you from your positions. Now that you're back, I think Julie should be acting AA, and I should go back to my previous role as P3 director. I'm not trying to shirk responsibility by saying this, and I will stay in this role as long as needed—or at least until they kick me out. But I want you to know that I know that you should be the ones leading the bureau, and I'm looking forward to getting back to that arrangement as soon as possible."

With that, I shut up. I had just dropped a lot on them, and I didn't know how they would react.

Julie was the one to respond for the group, ever ready to lead. She acknowledged how difficult the past two weeks must have been for us, as they had been for her and the others on administrative leave. She had many questions about how we had prioritized the essential staffing list, and why some individuals had been included while others were left off. She did not agree with my categorization of our job as grave digging, nor did she accept my conclusion that we should no longer make lists to facilitate the destruction of our agency.

"We need to be strategic," she said. "We need to help them understand why they need us. Fighting them will get us nowhere. We need to make ourselves indispensable." Despite being an early victim of DOGE's indiscriminate vengeance herself, I was amazed by how quickly she was back to "We're here to serve."

On the topic of leading the bureau, it was clear that Julie had already been making calls about this. She said that the formal process to designate her to the position of acting assistant administrator would be complicated, at least in the short term. In the meantime, the exact titles did not matter; we would all need to work as a team. Still, something would need to be done, she said, because it would be inappropriate for her and the other senior leaders to report to officials at a lower pay grade. Given the dire circumstances in which we found ourselves, I was a bit surprised to hear her concern with proper reporting channels, but I chalked it up to her unremitting attention to detail.

As the meeting wrapped up, I allowed myself one last look at the rooftop where the USAID flag continued to billow in the winter wind. Then I said goodbye to my colleagues and headed out, hoping to catch the second half of my daughter's soccer game that afternoon.

As I made my way across town, I reflected that the meeting had left me with an uneasy feeling. I had known things would change with Julie back at work, but now I wondered if she and I saw eye to eye on how to engage with the political leadership, and what it might mean if we didn't.

14.

The Mystery Man (Day 22)

On Monday, February 10, the USAID leadership moved its operations out of the Reagan Building for good, setting up shop at the State Department headquarters in the Foggy Bottom neighborhood of Washington. On the ground floor, several conference rooms in and around the Dean Acheson Auditorium—where twenty-two years earlier President Bush had presided over the PEPFAR signing ceremony—were designated for the various Co-ordination Support Team subgroups in their efforts to disassemble USAID.

That morning, as Julie and the deputies worked on reinstating their system access, Ramona and I made our way to Foggy Bottom. Entering the Programs Group conference room, I noticed that someone had written the Wi-Fi password on a whiteboard: "USAIDNextGen." I wondered whose mean-spirited idea it had been to force USAID staff to use that login to participate in an effort to ensure there would be no next generation of USAID.

I sat down and typed the password in on my laptop, thinking to myself, *Let the grave digging begin.*

The Programs Group's membership had grown somewhat from the small team that had gathered initially on Friday. The newcomers included program officers, legal advisors, and financial analysts, all of whom would periodically come and go, none of whom were ever introduced. In one corner of the conference room, a heavyset bald man with a tired frown and glasses, who I pegged for a political appointee, leaned back in his chair silently throughout the meeting.

We were grappling with a growing list of potentially fatal obstacles to restarting lifesaving activities. All of them had been intentionally erected by DOGE and the political appointees, blocking us from what had been routine operations merely three weeks earlier. By now, using the authority that Joel Borkert had granted me to approve global health activities under the waiver, my team had identified nearly two dozen lifesaving activities that needed to restart right away. Yet none of the activities had actually resumed.

A key problem was that USAID's financial system was broken—not figuratively, but literally—preventing funds from flowing to contractors to resume their work. Ramona and I, along with the other career staff in attendance, spent the morning trying to explain, in increasingly simplistic terms, how the agency's complex financial systems functioned and why they weren't working now.

USAID contractors received funds either in reimbursement for their expenses, or as a short-term advance to cover their costs. In either case, we did not simply send money to contractors whenever they claimed they needed it. Prior to authorizing payments, project managers first assessed the proposed expenses to ensure USAID only paid for the goods and services it needed under the contract, and only then could contracting officers approve the payments. This verification process was a key safeguard against waste, fraud, and abuse. But now DOGE had restricted access, and the officials who assess and approve payments to contractors were shut out of the system. To restart lifesaving activities, we explained, USAID needed to provide funding to our contractors, which the financial system did not allow without first verifying that the expenses were legitimate. Ironically, in a move they claimed was necessary to prevent waste, fraud, and abuse, DOGE had locked out the individuals whose job it was to ensure the expenses were justified, a prerequisite to allowing the funds to flow.

All the while, the political appointees stared at us blankly—Tim Meisburger and Meghan Hanson with furrowed brows, and the rotund mystery man in the corner repeatedly detaching and reattaching his magnetic, pull-apart glasses from the bridge of his nose, as if there might be a smudge on his lenses that was the source of his confusion.

Eventually, we brought in a finance director from the State Department to provide a clearer explanation of the challenges that were holding up payments. He was blunt. "The reason that funds are not flowing is that DOGE has shut off access to the payments system," he said. "The certifying officials who verify that payments should be made to contractors are no longer able to do that. Right now the only people with access to the system are three guys from DOGE, and they would have no idea whether to authorize payments or not. If you want funds to flow, the solution is to have DOGE reinstate access."

But no one from DOGE was part of the Programs Group, or of any of the CST groups, and they showed no willingness to reinstate system access. They had shut it down on purpose. We would have to come up with a makeshift, work-around solution.

There was a system that worked, but DOGE broke it. This explanation summed up most of the challenges we would face in the Programs Group. Dozens, if not hundreds, of staff members across the various CST groups spent days, sometimes even weeks, trying to fix problems that could have been solved with a few keyboard strokes. What we came up with never worked as well as the system we had before—if it worked at all, which it often did not.

During a break in the meeting, Ramona and I introduced ourselves to the mystery man. He was Mark Lloyd, Trump's pick to lead USAID's Bureau for Conflict Prevention and Stabilization. Although he had sat silently all morning, he was excited to talk now. Mark had served at USAID during the first Trump administration as the agency's religious freedom advisor, an appointment that had drawn criticism from within and outside the agency due to his substantial public history of Islamophobic rhetoric (he once called Islam "a barbaric cult" and advocated for forcing people to eat bacon before they can purchase firearms).

When I asked what he thought about dismantling the agency where he had just been appointed as a leader, Mark's eyes lit up. He described with excitement his deep-seated distrust and animosity toward USAID and its staff. During his first stint at the agency, he told me, the civil service employees had been horrible to him, leaking terrible things about him to the press to make him look like a bigot. He was *not* Islamophobic, he interjected. Then, raising an eyebrow, he added: "I just don't like people who want to blow us up."

He went on, describing in a low, dramatic tone how the career staff had wronged him, just like they had wronged his friends Tim Meisburger and Pete Marocco, who had also served at USAID during the first Trump term. "They were awful," he said of the agency's civil servants, bringing his face very close to mine. "They tracked down my family and sent pictures of my son's house to threaten me. And then they killed my dog!"

I gasped, and he continued. "So, yeah, when Pete called me up and asked if I wanted to come back to USAID, I said, 'Yes, sir, I have a list.'"

I was speechless. I did not believe that USAID staff had threatened Mark's family or killed his dog. But most of my disbelief was reserved for my dawning realization that the political appointees in charge of USAID were not just tearing down our agency without care or concern for the damage they were doing. At least some of them were out for revenge and actually enjoying themselves.

On our way out of the building that evening, I told Ramona that I was just glad that Mark wasn't the political appointee overseeing global health. "Careful, Nick," she said, half joking. "At this rate, by tomorrow, maybe he will be."

15.

False Narrative (Days 23–25)

Tuesday, February 11, was a particularly bad day. DOGE issued a new tranche of contracts that they wanted canceled, and Jami Rodgers again ordered USAID's contracting officers to terminate them immediately. Once more I protested, insisting to Jami and Nadeem that my staff and I at least review any GH contracts to ensure that they were not needed to implement lifesaving activities.

While we were reviewing those contracts, I received an email from Jeremy Lewin at DOGE. Someone had told him that I was slowing down the process of terminating contracts by conducting my own reviews, and he was not having it. "This is delaying the timely processing of these termination notices and is unacceptable," he wrote. "As Jami's instructions made clear, the awards in each of the tranches cleared for termination have been extensively reviewed by State F, Secretary/Acting Administrator Rubio, and approved for termination by the full chain of command."

But the contracts had not been "extensively reviewed" by the State Department or by Rubio. There was no feasible way for them to have been reviewed for content without anyone talking to the contracting officers or the program managers who knew what the contracts actually did. It was Jeremy himself who had affirmed to Rubio that "none of these obligations relate to the operation of key waivered or excepted programs," even though he had no way of knowing whether this was true. In fact, my team had so

far identified at least one GH contract that Jeremy had slated for termination that I had already approved to resume under Rubio's waiver.

I told Jeremy that I was not trying to hold up his termination plans,
only to provide him with information about which contracts the waiver
applied to. Still, I recognized that "the decision whether to terminate the
awards or not is entirely up to the front office." He never responded, but
the damage had been done. The termination orders would keep coming,
but that was the last time my staff and I were allowed to see the lists before
the contracts were terminated.

As if this were not enough, I received another concerning email that
morning. It was from Joel Borkert and, innocuous as it sounded, it was the
fulfillment of Ramona's dark prediction: "Mark Lloyd is going to provide
you some political help and oversight as we move forward. Please run all
issues through him."

And just like that, I was reporting to someone who believed that
USAID's civil servants were dog murderers.

The next setback that gloomy Tuesday was arguably the most concerning. As my team pressed ahead with identifying activities to restart, Joel
told me that I was approving too many. By now I had approved thirty
activities—thirty among the thousands that we had been implementing
globally—that were the highest priority. I had reviewed each one to ensure there was a clear case for why it was needed to avert the loss of lives
within the next thirty days, and rejected, painful as it was, those that had
not made a strong-enough justification. What remained were critical drugs
and supplies to combat Ebola, mpox, Marburg virus, TB, malaria, HIV,
vaccinations for other deadly diseases like cholera and polio, and lifesaving
medical services for childbirth, such as cesarean sections and surgeries to
address postpartum hemorrhage.

"I told you it had to be draconian," Joel admonished me. That word
again. It was at least the third time I'd heard him use it.

I was at a loss. I knew that Pete Marocco, Jeremy Lewin, and the others
were suspicious that the agency's staff would try to use the waiver as a loophole
to approve noncritical activities. That was why I had strictly reviewed the var-

ious submissions, only approving those I could confidently defend as meeting the definition of "lifesaving." Now, without even looking at which activities I had approved, they were saying it was too many. This was a new restriction; the waiver itself had said that lifesaving activities should be restarted, not that there would be a cap on how many. I reported back to my team what Joel had said. Julie suggested that we needed to find a way to be more restrictive in our review, and that maybe there was a way for us to tighten our definition.

Then things got worse. I received an email from Paul Seong, the career foreign service officer who was now embedded in the agency's front office as a senior advisor. Copying Joel and Meghan Hanson, Paul directed me to "hold off on any more approvals" of lifesaving activities. I forwarded Paul's email widely, including within GH and to other pertinent bureaus, alerting the broader agency that my approval authority had suddenly been revoked.

Paul's email felt like a breaking point. I was already thoroughly skeptical of the administration's commitment to saving lives by implementing the waiver. Since the previous week, when Joel signed the memo authorizing me to restart some programs, I had approved thirty urgent activities, and yet none were actually underway. My repeated alerts about the broken payment system had gone unheeded, and it was just a matter of time before people would start dying, if they hadn't already. Yet there was no urgency—no action whatsoever—from our political leaders to fix the problem. Now my authority to approve lifesaving activities had been revoked. If I couldn't approve the activities, the funding challenge would be an academic exercise, with no hope of resuming our most critical work.

At almost that exact moment, as I sat dejectedly in a State Department conference room contemplating the dimming hopes for our programs, Elon Musk was holding a press conference a few blocks away, in the Oval Office alongside President Trump. Dressed all in black, from his MAGA hat to his tee and blazer, Musk updated reporters about DOGE's conquests at USAID and other agencies. With his son X sitting on his shoulders, Musk was asked whether cuts at USAID were putting Americans at risk from the spread of infectious diseases. He denied it. "We have turned on funding for Ebola prevention, and for HIV prevention," he said reassuringly. Watching the clip a few hours later, I was furious. Not only had the Trump administration removed our ability to restart lifesaving activities earlier that day, but Elon Musk was standing in the Oval Office lying about it.

Watching Musk deceive the American public about the fact that his team was actively preventing USAID from mounting a response to an ongoing Ebola outbreak, something inside me snapped. I suddenly felt that I needed to do something—anything—before it was too late. But what could I do? The administration I worked for did not care about the lives it was putting at risk as it ruthlessly tore down the agency to which I and so many others had devoted years of hard work. I felt powerless. Then I remembered that the only reason the political appointees had set up the Programs Group in the first place was that they had been seeing negative stories in the press about food and medicine expiring in warehouses. I thought maybe there was a way to get their attention.

I had never done anything like this before, but I was desperate. I called my brother, David, to whom I often went for advice and guidance. On this matter he could also help me in a professional capacity. After more than fifteen years as a reporter for various small newspapers and then at *The Wall Street Journal*, he was now an editor at *The New York Times*. I told him I had evidence that USAID was blocking lifesaving aid, despite Rubio's waiver. David explained that standards of journalism barred him from being involved with reporting related to his brother, and that all he could do was give me the contact information for his colleague who was reporting on USAID.

That was all I needed. I explained my role at USAID to the *Times* reporter, and how I knew that Musk had been lying at the White House that day. I shared the email that Paul Seong had sent me freezing our ability to restart USAID's lifesaving programs, along with other emails documenting that the funds for Ebola still had not moved.

The next day, the *Times* published an article with the headline "Lifesaving Aid Remains Halted Worldwide Despite Rubio's Promise," which reported: "When Secretary of State Marco Rubio announced last month that lifesaving humanitarian work would be exempt from a freeze on foreign aid, global health workers breathed a collective sigh of relief. But a new directive has put such exemptions on hold." It then quoted Paul's email to me to "hold off on any more approvals," and confirmed that the Ebola prevention activities had not restarted, despite Elon Musk's claim in the Oval Office.

As I walked into the State Department for that morning's meeting of the Programs Group, I was terrified. And I was not surprised when, around ten o'clock, I was told that Joel Borkert wanted to see me. Julie had accompanied me to Foggy Bottom that morning, and the two of us walked to a corner of the hallway where Joel had gathered several of his lieutenants. I knew exactly what was coming, and reminded myself, to little avail, of my vow to not be intimidated.

"Why am I reading in *The New York Times* that the waiver is on hold?" he began angrily. "Pete is furious. Now he has to explain why the lifesaving work is not happening, when he's been telling everyone that it's in place. I don't understand why the media would be saying that we paused the waiver. We never paused the waiver."

"I saw the article," I said carefully. "I think they're referring to the email, the one Paul sent yesterday, saying to hold off on any more approvals." He seemed to have no idea what I was talking about.

"There never was a pause," said Laken Rapier, the political appointee responsible for press at USAID. Then she shouted it: "THERE NEVER WAS A PAUSE!"

I was confused. There had been a pause. Did these people not read their emails? Was Paul going to speak up and correct them? No chance. It was back to me.

"I think there was a pause," I said timidly. "Let me bring up the email for you." And so I did, passing my phone around to the group of angry faces, who read the message one by one. It was clear as day: "Hold off on any more approvals." There was a pause.

Then Tim Meisburger, the political appointee who had derailed a meeting last week in search of dry-erase markers, jumped in: "The more important question is, who leaked the email to the press? I'm so sick of people at this agency feeling like they can just leak anything they don't like to the press. Now we're standing out here in the hallway arguing about pauses or no pauses, when we should be in there saving lives!" (As if saving lives was what was happening in the conference rooms.)

Tim was irate, and the group agreed enthusiastically. He went on. "Laken, you need to find the leaker. Get together with the kids with the red sneakers," he said, referring to the DOGE team, "and have them find out who leaked this."

Mark Lloyd chimed in, echoing Tim. "We need to root out the leaker. And when we find out who leaked this—and we *will* find out," he said, wagging a finger in my direction, "they are going to be fired and prosecuted!"

Laken concurred: "They're already working on the forensics. But right now, we need to issue a response." She turned to me. "I want you to get a memo out ASAP to counter this false narrative in the press that there was a pause. It needs to say very clearly that there *never was a pause.*"

"And it should also say that any further leaks will be met with harsh discipline," said Tim. "I like what Mark said about prosecution. I don't know if we can include that, but we should if we can."

Julie, unaware that the leaker was standing beside her, tried to run damage control. "We hate the leaks as much as you do," she told the politicals. "It hurts our credibility, and hurts our trust with you. I don't know who leaked this email, but we will make sure that all GH staff get the message that leaking to the press is unacceptable. In the meantime, we'll get to work on that memo right away."

"Can I clarify one thing on the new memo?" I asked hesitantly. This was my opportunity to get the political team on the record. "I assume it should also specify how we approve new activities under the waiver, right? Should we use the same process we were using before the pause, that—"

"THERE NEVER WAS A PAUSE!" Laken interrupted.

"Sorry," I said. "I just mean: Should we include the same process from the last memo again, so staff will know that I'm still approving new global health activities that meet the definition of lifesaving?"

"Yes," said Joel. "Let's do that. And we need it fast."

Fast sounded great to me, too.

I drafted the memo that afternoon. Possibly the worst memo I ever wrote, I held my nose and typed the phrases the political appointees had insisted upon, even though I knew they were not true. Even the memo's subject line was inaccurate: "Clarifying that Global Health (GH) programming under the lifesaving humanitarian assistance waiver has continued uninterrupted and was never paused." The body of the memo was no less problematic, beginning by maligning the media: "The purpose of this memo is to correct a false narrative in the press, and provide clarity for staff on external communications." It went on to remind staff that "unauthorized engagement externally with the press or others is subject to discipline, including dismissal," which felt especially odious coming from me considering how this memo originated.

But following the one-page exercise in revisionist history, I included as an attachment the "Lifesaving Humanitarian Assistance Process for GH," which clearly reinstated my authority to restart frozen activities that were needed to save lives.

The next morning, as I was sitting in a Programs Group meeting led by Tim Meisburger, Joel approved the memo for me to send out to the workforce as the acting assistant administrator for global health. I hesitated, dreading the thought of circulating this repugnant memo under my name. At the same time, the memo's attachment was the key to resuming our work, and I knew it was worth the humiliation of owning the words I had written.

Just as I was about to hit send, Tim told me to wait. He wanted the memo to come from a political appointee rather than a career official. I watched as he opened the memo on his laptop—his Google icon joining mine at the top of the document—and he changed the "from" line where my name and title were listed to read simply "Mark Lloyd." I mentioned that it might be confusing to the GH staff—the memo's intended audience—if the memo defining the process for approving global health activities were to come from Mark, the assistant to the administrator for conflict prevention and stabilization, rather than from the head of GH. To address this, Tim edited further, adding "performing the duties of Assistant Administrator, Bureau for Global Health" next to Mark's name.

Tim had already demonstrated his disregard for agency protocols, so I was not surprised that he was comfortable making edits to a memo after it had been approved. But the change itself was shocking: As the assistant to the administrator for humanitarian assistance, Tim had no authority to delegate the duties related to global health, a wholly separate and independent bureau from the one he led.

When he finished making the change, Tim told me to send it. I did.

At least the pause was over, and I could start approving new activities again. But this small victory felt precarious; one step forward, two huge slides back.

16.

Losing Ground (Days 26–29)

It had been nearly a month since President Trump's order on Inauguration Day to pause foreign assistance, and the fatal consequences of freezing USAID's global health programs were starting to emerge. Across Africa, health facilities were experiencing shortages of antiretroviral drugs, and patients were rationing HIV medications or buying low-quality alternatives on the black market. Health ministries were reporting unmanageably long lines at clinics and hospitals, and patients were being turned away without receiving test results or treatment. At certain clinics in Uganda, as many as 25 percent of babies were being born with HIV due to interruptions to treatment that prevents mother-to-child transmission. That number had been near zero just weeks earlier.

From South Sudan came reports of the first deaths resulting from interruptions to USAID-supported health services. Community health workers, many of whom provided HIV services to hundreds of people in communities without access to health facilities, had been fired in late January, cutting off patients from the treatment and services that were keeping them alive. Without their antiretroviral drugs, patients' health began to deteriorate quickly, and by mid-February people were starting to die.

After my authority to restart lifesaving activities was restored on Thursday, February 13, I once again turned my attention to getting our most critical programs back online. I wrote to Brian Frantz, the head of the Bureau for Africa, asking for his help to prioritize restarting lifesaving health activities in his region. We needed each USAID mission to identify the contracts that needed to be restarted to limit loss of life in its country. But I quickly learned that our capabilities to deliver lifesaving aid were cracking under the pressure—and it was not only our broken payment system that was hampering our ability to proceed.

The previous week's news that the entire staff of USAID would soon be placed on administrative leave, and that Americans stationed abroad would be sent back to the U.S. imminently, had been especially jarring for the agency's thousands of overseas staff. The court's temporary restraining order, which promised only a week's reprieve, did little to quell their fears. Now, as we in Washington were desperate to save our vital programs, Brian made the difficult but entirely understandable decision to prioritize the safe return of his foreign service officers to the U.S. over the urgent need to restart lifesaving programs. He responded that, for his bureau:

> The top near-term priority is figuring out how we organize ourselves to ensure the safety of our personnel in the field and prepare to undertake the massive repatriation effort that we expect to get underway shortly after virtually the entire Bureau is placed on admin leave and goes dark. As such, we are generally NOT going to be able to execute on any of the waivers to lift stop-work orders on priority programs managed in the field until some of this dust settles a little bit. I know you are under pressure to get some of those programs moving again . . . but for the moment, I cannot in good conscience ask our Missions to prioritize resuming programs that they manage until we have a handle on the personnel stuff.

It was heart-wrenching to read Brian's message. In addition to the growing catastrophe resulting from the interruption to our regular health programs in Africa, Brian's team was closely monitoring the Ebola outbreak in Uganda as well as an outbreak of Marburg virus in Tanzania. He knew that failing to prioritize health programs would have lethal repercussions, but he was in an impossible position. It was easy for me to prioritize the health programs, but GH was not directly responsible for USAID's overseas staff. As the head of the Africa Bureau, that was Brian's responsibility, and I completely understood his decision, painful as it must have been.

Even with their primary focus shifted to repatriation, however, the mission staff came through. Foreign service officers understood the urgency of restarting these lifesaving health programs, and they continued to send requests for contracts to be turned on, even as they tended to their own affairs, making arrangements for medical procedures, school admissions, transfers of pets, lease cancellations, and everything else. Most important, the missions were staffed primarily by local experts from the host country, whose commitment to restarting health programs in their home country never wavered, even amid the deepening chaos.

As additional contracts with lifesaving activities were identified, my team reviewed them to ensure that I approved only the most essential programs to be restarted. But on Friday, February 14, as I prepared to approve another two dozen critical activities, my authority was revoked yet again, just twenty-four hours after it had been restored. That morning, the State Department released new "Foreign Assistance Pause" guidance, which prescribed a new, more restrictive process for approving lifesaving activities, delegating this authority solely to Ken Jackson for all USAID activities. I now needed to convince Ken—the same person who the week before had admitted to knowing nothing about USAID's global health work—before any lifesaving services could be restored.

When the Programs Group met that Friday, I brought with me a long list of agenda items. The stated purpose of the Programs Group was to resolve issues related to the implementation of the lifesaving humanitarian assistance waiver. But not only had we failed to make any progress on the challenges we were already facing—the broken payment system, the haphazard termination of contracts needed to provide critical services— the administration was erecting new roadblocks. Tim Meisburger, the self-proclaimed head of the Programs Group, promised the frustrated career officials that he would bring these problems to the attention of senior leaders at USAID, the State Department, and DOGE. But when we identified obstacles that were preventing us from resuming lifesaving work, it became clear that his offer of support was no more than lip service.

The insincerity of Tim's promise was exposed when we alerted him to the fact that GH project managers were receiving a daily torrent of concerns and complaints from our contractors abroad. They had been approved to restart lifesaving activities, but were unable to access the funds they needed to do so. Several contractors sent worried reminders about overdue unpaid invoices. Without access to funds, they were unable to implement the lifesaving activities that had been approved and would be forced to shut down entirely.

Our contractors were usually eager to please USAID, with an eye toward winning future contracts, but as time passed without any funds being transferred, even our most long-standing partners could not sugarcoat the reality that continuing their work had become impossible. For example, one major supplier of lifesaving medicines around the world warned that its entire inventory of drugs was at risk without new funding: "Suppliers and logistics companies are not confident that we will pay them and do not want to release orders to our custody or take on additional work required to safeguard these commodities without absolute surety of payment." Despite our pleas and warnings, Tim failed to take action.

The Ebola outbreak in Uganda was a clear example of the problem. Despite our having approved contractors to begin response activities, no work had started, as USAID's partners on-site had not received any funding to do the work. I told Tim that Elon Musk had publicly announced that he had "turned on funding for Ebola prevention," which simply was not true.

"I assume Musk's statement means that he *wants* Ebola prevention activities to restart," I said, putting a generous spin on what was happening. "Can you please ask DOGE to at least process payments for the Ebola response?"

I followed up with an email to Tim, Joel Borkert, and Mark Lloyd to express the urgency of processing payments for the Ebola response:

> At this time, our implementing partners are still unable to access funds. . . . For example, IOM [the International Organization for

Migration] is positioned to bolster Ebola screening at Entebbe International Airport in Uganda, but has not commenced as they are not able to access advance funds. This is leading to unscreened passengers traveling internationally, potentially onwards to the U.S.

If the access to funding is not resolved imminently, we stand to lose crucial ground on the response, threatening lives in the US and abroad. . . . Every day that we lose in this response is one more day that increases the risk of this outbreak and the threat to our national security.

Elon Musk publicly confirmed from the Oval Office about USAID that "we have, for example, turned on funding for Ebola prevention. . . ." This hasn't actually happened for USAID-funded Ebola activities due to this payment obstacle.

Tim's response to my email was unsympathetic. Rather than help resolve the problem, as he had offered, he shifted the blame to the unpaid contractor. He wrote: "So, this is one of the most critical health emergencies in the world, but the International Organization for Migration, which has capacity on the ground, will not provide this screening because the US has a short-term cash flow problem? I'm really appalled."

I was not surprised that Tim was unwilling to help find a solution, and I was troubled by his euphemism of a "short-term cash flow problem," when what he really meant was the administration's refusal to pay for contracted services. But I knew there was no use in arguing that point. And so I responded to provide additional context on the partner's financial circumstances, hoping I might still be able to convince him to help:

We share your concerns about IOM starting activities, but are not in position to force them without providing access to funding as provided in the agreement terms. Additional details from the IOM [project manager] on the problem:

IOM has a massive cash flow issue right now—and in normal times it doesn't have the sort of cash flow that other PIOs [public international

organizations] manage. IOM needs to be able to submit reimbursement
requests every 7 days to stay solvent. . . .

I know that the team is scrambling to find any other possible
options. At the same time, USAID has approved IOM to conduct these
activities and should allow payment per our contractual agreement. In
the interim, the lack of payment is hampering our ebola response.

Tim never responded.

Once again, it was a court decision, not any action taken by USAID's
political leadership, that kept hopes for our programs alive. In a lawsuit
brought by several of the agency's contractors, another federal judge issued
a temporary restraining order, this one prohibiting the administration from
pausing the disbursement of foreign assistance funds. The order also barred
the administration from "issuing, implementing, enforcing, or otherwise
giving effect to terminations, suspensions, or stop-work orders in connection with any contracts, grants, cooperative agreements, loans, or other
federal foreign assistance award that was in existence as of January 19, 2025."

In response to the ruling, Jami Rodgers in our contracting office issued
new guidance on Monday, February 17, to all USAID contracting officers
worldwide: "Until further notice, all Contracting and Agreement Officers
should not enforce any Agency directive issued under executive order 14169
and the Secretary's implementing memorandum that requires the general-
ized stop work, suspension, or pause of Agency contracts, grants or other
federal assistance awards."

This sounded promising. By my reading, it meant that all our global
health work would be able to restart, not just the limited subset of "lifesaving activities." Moreover, it would mean an end, at least temporarily, to
DOGE sending lists of contracts to be terminated. I sent a message to Jami
for clarification, and he confirmed: "Yes, this is legalese to lift stop-work
orders. We will have more guidance tomorrow."

I was ecstatic. This was the reprieve we had been hoping for. The administration could continue its plan to review our programs and make policy decisions related to what they would prioritize in foreign aid moving forward. But in the meantime, our programs would continue. Our work would be unfrozen and our contracts would no longer be at the whim of Jeremy Lewin's arbitrary termination lists. This one ruling would save countless lives and steer us back toward the path of rational policymaking.

But my excitement was short-lived. It had not occurred to me that the administration would simply ignore the binding legal order of a court, but that is exactly what happened. USAID's political leaders did not lift the pause on funding, as the judge had ordered, nor did they rescind the stop-work orders or contract terminations.

The additional guidance that Jami had promised to lift the foreign assistance pause never arrived. Instead, Jeremy brazenly flouted the intent of the court order during a meeting of the entire Coordination Support Team. He explained that the court's ruling was misguided and would have the opposite of its intended effect. Relying on language in the court's ruling that "nothing in this order shall prohibit the [administration] from enforcing the terms of contracts or grants," Jeremy stated that all USAID contracts included a "termination for convenience" provision, and therefore the awards could still be terminated despite the court order. Because USAID was now barred from pausing foreign assistance funding, he reasoned, the only way to ensure that contractors were not receiving improper payments or conducting activities that failed to align with the president's policy priorities was to exercise the termination for convenience clause en masse.

Despite the court's ruling, the outlook for our programs was bleaker than ever.

17.

Happy Birthday (Days 30–31)

Starting on Tuesday, February 18, what remained of USAID headquarters moved again, this time downtown to a leased office building on 12th Street Northwest, where the Bureau for Humanitarian Assistance had been located. As the political appointees settled into abandoned offices on the eighth and ninth floors, the Coordination Support Team continued its mission to shut down USAID, operating from a row of nondescript conference rooms in the building's basement.

While most GH staff remained at home, I spent my days in the Programs Group conference room along with Julie, Nida, Ramona, Natalia, and deputy assistant administrators Carmen Coles and Han Kang, all of us grappling with the deteriorating status of our health programs. From our new digs, once a day our small GH contingent would take the elevator up to Mark Lloyd's office, where we would repeat our requests for help in restarting the lifesaving activities that remained frozen. Those meetings were excruciating. Each day we recited the same pleas, and each day Mark would make a point of acting concerned—he would unsnap his magnetic glasses, rub his eyes in consternation, and theatrically proclaim, in apparent solidarity, that "we have to save the babies." But he never took the step of advocating on our behalf with his bosses at USAID, the State Department, or DOGE.

In the days since the revocation of my authority to restart essential programs, the agency had not approved a single lifesaving activity to be resumed. Mark was skeptical of the activities we were proposing, asking for increasingly detailed justifications for why they were absolutely critical. He did not understand our programs, and he did not trust us when we tried to describe them, so we were at a stalemate. Looking for a solution, Julie proposed that we could beef up our justifications by specifying the number of lives that would be saved by each activity we were requesting to restart. Mark seemed pleased with this idea. I was suspicious that he would have agreed to any plan that resulted in us going back to rework our requests and him not green-lighting any activities. I was concerned that the more details we provided on each activity the less likely Mark would be to read them.

Nonetheless, our teams set to work on meticulously detailing the exact number of lives affected by each activity. The justification sections in our requests grew and grew, as did the time and effort that went into preparing them. Unfortunately, my concerns were confirmed: Even with the additional quantification effort, Mark did not sign off on a single activity for approval.

We didn't seem to be making any progress, but Julie believed that our daily meetings with Mark were productive. As we listened to him waste the allotted time retelling the same stories—day after day, he would recount tales of trips he had taken to Guatemala and Haiti where he had once seen health programs, the time he'd had to fire people from the business he ran ("Now, *those* were hard workers," a not-so-subtle dig at federal employees), or his occasional middle-of-the-night bladder challenges—Julie was convinced that by nodding and smiling along we were building trust and rapport, an investment that would pay off in time.

During our daily check-in on Wednesday, February 19, after we ran through our growing list of stalled programs, Mark told us that it was his birthday. After the meeting, as the GH team reassembled in our basement conference room, Julie proposed that we buy a cake and sing "Happy Birthday" to Mark at the end of the day.

My stomach turned at the thought, and I told Julie that I would not sing to Mark.

"Why not?" she asked. "If this were any other administration, we would sing 'Happy Birthday' to our political appointee."

That was true, but we had never before had political appointees who demonstrated such callous indifference to our staff and our programs. Julie began to negotiate with me—*How about a cupcake and a candle, but no song?*—but a Programs Group meeting started before we could agree, and she mercifully did not bring up the topic again.

In the basement on 12th Street, we were once again planning for the vast majority of USAID personnel to be placed on administrative leave as soon as the temporary restraining order was lifted, presumably by the end of the week, leaving only a few "essential" staff to remain at the agency. For the second time in two weeks, we were asked to provide a rank-ordered list of GH employees, determining who would stay to carry out our critical functions and who would be let go.

Although I had vowed to myself that I would refuse any future directives to prepare lists that would cut staff to levels below what was needed to accomplish our work, Julie dove into the task. That is not to say that she agreed with it; she knew as well as I did that cutting our staffing levels to below 10 percent of what they had been a month earlier would preclude us from implementing and managing our programs, putting millions of lives at risk. But she was able to compartmentalize her anguish in order to ensure that what little remained of our bureau was the strongest team possible.

Natalia warned us that this exercise likely ran afoul of agency and government-wide personnel rules. Over the course of her fifteen-year career at USAID, she had developed an encyclopedic familiarity with the agency's rules and procedures. She had helped draft the previous essential staffing list two weeks earlier, but this was different. The first time we were directed to rank our staff, the long-term fate of those who did not make the essential list was unclear. This time there was no question. The list was intended to capture a new, final-state footprint for the agency, with the small list of essential employees remaining and everyone else permanently fired.

Julie dismissed Natalia's concerns, reasoning that we had no choice but to comply with the directive. I argued that we could choose not to provide a list, even if it cost us our jobs. There is always a choice. Julie asked me if this was the hill I wanted to die on.

"Look," she said, "I'm grieving for our lost staff, too. I hate that we are in this position. But if we don't do it, they'll just push us out and find someone else who will. My hope is that this list is just a start that we can build back from. The good news is that we can build a great list, a team of rock stars! If there is any chance of saving even parts of our work, this team can do it."

I reflected on Julie's ability to accept that we faced a new reality and to seamlessly pivot from a past that had been so unreasonably stripped away. While I was ready to fight, she was convinced that, if we were strategic, we could earn the support of the political appointees and preserve core components of our work. Regretfully, over the course of that week, I crossed the red line I had drawn for myself, and I helped Julie prepare the list. I had spent my career carrying out the directives of political appointees, and I guess I found it a hard habit to break. Plus, I was accustomed to helping Julie, my boss until three weeks prior, with her priorities. Whatever the reason, it was only the latest example of my failure to stick to my principles as I continued to help dig USAID's grave.

There was no longer any question that USAID was being dismantled, and that most of our programs and staff were being slashed. But the political appointees were dangling a thread of hope that our most critical work could be saved, along with a small core team to manage it. In our daily meetings with Mark, Julie and I provided updates on the list. He was excited and congratulatory that our latest number, sixty-two, was lower than the seventy-seven I had offered the last time we had been asked for a rank-ordered list. He implied that the worst would soon be over.

"Let's face it," he said. "The *Titanic* is going down. The question is, how do we make sure that the right people are in the lifeboat?"

Mark used the lifeboat metaphor repeatedly whenever he referred to the short list of essential personnel, at times stretching the comparison beyond its rational limits. ("Let's make sure our lifeboat is not full of cannibals.") I quickly grew to hate it.

Julie picked up on Mark's lifeboat metaphor, reusing it liberally as she tried to convince herself and the team that those of us on the essential list would be spared the fate of the rest of the agency. If we could get the right list, she reasoned, and then work harder than ever to prove our team's value, we could still save key parts of our work.

I was far more skeptical. I did not believe that Mark, or any of the political appointees, were interested in saving any part of USAID, or its staff. Even if he was, I doubted that he held any sway over Pete Marocco—not to mention DOGE—in advocating for global health in the face of their quest for the agency's complete demolition. I had seen no evidence so far to suggest that Mark was willing or able to intervene on behalf of our most urgent programming challenges. I was not holding my breath for him to save the day now. Regardless, whether our essential staff list would be a lifeboat for global health programs or merely an elongation of our grave-digging assignment, in either case it meant the same thing for the employees who were not on it: Their careers at USAID were over.

As Julie and I continued to work on the list, I went through every rationalization I could think of: *I am following a directive from our political leadership. If I don't do it, someone else will. USAID is being dismantled anyway.* But the truth is, I sent the list of names to Mark Lloyd, directly resulting in hundreds of my colleagues losing their jobs. This was the choice I made, and it weighs heavily on me to this day.

With DOGE still refusing to release payments to contractors, and with no support from the political appointees, our efforts to respond to the Ebola outbreak in Uganda continued to sputter. But even without access to funds, we had one other avenue to support the healthcare workers on the ground who were fighting the outbreak. As part of our global health security strategy, USAID had already purchased twenty-seven thousand sets of personal protective equipment that were prepositioned at a nearby warehouse in Kenya, ready for use in case of an outbreak, like this one, in the region.

PPE—the surgical gloves, masks, hoods, and gowns that protect health workers from exposure and infection—is one of the most important and time-sensitive needs during an Ebola outbreak. When health workers don't have early access to PPE, Ebola is likely to spread rapidly among the doctors and nurses on the front lines as they scramble to identify, diagnose, and treat the sick. This often results in the decimation of the health workforce through high rates of infection and sickness, incapacitating the very people who are needed most to respond to the outbreak, and the crisis deepens.

The large stockpile of PPE was located a short drive from the Ugandan border, which meant that these critical supplies could be delivered within only a few hours. But the outbreak was now in its third week, and still the PPE sat idly in the warehouse in Kenya. The problem was that the warehouse was owned and operated by the World Health Organization, from which the Trump administration was in the process of withdrawing. In another executive order issued on January 20, Trump had paused the transfer of "funds, support, or resources to the WHO."

Although USAID had already paid for the PPE, the lawyers at the agency and at the State Department had interpreted the executive order to prevent us from authorizing the nominal fee to the WHO to deliver the supplies to the Ugandan authorities. When we requested Joel Borkert's support to urgently move the PPE back on February 3, he had promised to help find a solution. In our meeting that same week with the National Security Council about the outbreak, I had urged the State Department to issue supplemental guidance on the executive order, authorizing exceptions to work with the WHO in emergency cases like this one. On February 11, I emailed Joel, along with Mark Lloyd and Ken Jackson, reminding them that we still had not received guidance or approval to move the PPE out of the warehouse, but I received no response. I raised the matter again in the Programs Group meeting with Tim and Mark on February 12, but there was still no progress.

In an effort to force the issue, I sent a memo to Pete Marocco on February 18, requesting his approval to engage with WHO for the limited purpose of moving the PPE into Uganda to respond to the Ebola outbreak.

The following day, Joel sent me an email at 6:03 p.m. He wrote that he was "confused about the WHO PPE issue. I've said multiple times there is no issue with using the PPE. I don't understand why I am getting a [memo] requesting this. I was under the impression this was done weeks ago based on my verbal directive in multiple meetings."

We then spoke by phone. I reminded Joel again that the PPE had not moved because we needed formal State Department approval due to the president's executive order on the U.S. withdrawal from the WHO. I told him that if he could just have Pete sign the memo, we could move the PPE immediately. He said he would call Pete and get back to me.

Joel called again around seven that evening. He had spoken to Pete, and he was absolutely sure that Pete would not sign the memo. But, Joel told me, Pete wanted the PPE to be used for the Ebola outbreak in Uganda. "You need to find another way to get it," he said. I told him that we could procure PPE from other sources, but it would likely add days or weeks to the timeline, as it would need to be transported from Europe or Asia. Plus, we had already paid for the PPE in the Kenyan warehouse.

"If we want to move the PPE quickly," I told him, "Marocco needs to just sign the memo. If he won't sign it, we'll need to buy more PPE somewhere else. That's going to take time and money."

"He's not going to sign it," Joel said flatly. Then he told me what he was going to do. "On behalf of Pete Marocco, I'm going to issue you an order right after this call. You will need to go get the PPE from the warehouse without engaging with WHO and get it to Uganda."

This was ridiculous. What was I supposed to do, fly to Kenya and break into the warehouse with a crowbar?

Apparently so. Three minutes later, Joel emailed me to confirm: "I just spoke with Mr. Marocco regarding the U.S. purchased and owned PPE in a WHO warehouse in Kenya. We are ordering you to pick up the PPE and deliver it to the necessary people and organizations in the region to respond to ongoing infectious disease outbreaks."

I studied Joel's email. I realized that he actually expected me, or my staff, to go to Kenya and take the PPE. There were so many reasons this was not legal, or feasible, I didn't even know where to start. At 7:43 p.m., another email came in. It was Pete Marocco replying to Joel's email: "Mark/Tim/Joel, Please take all necessary personnel actions in the event this is not completed in the next 12 hours."

It was nearly three in the morning in Kenya. I had twelve hours to somehow collect PPE from the WHO warehouse and get it to Uganda, or apparently I would be fired. And I was not authorized to talk to the WHO. I felt like I was in a reality show, except there were real lives at stake, not to mention my own job.

I called the Outbreak Response Team and explained the predicament. To their enormous credit, despite the late hour and preposterous scenario I presented, the team sprang into action, drafting alternative options, researching how quickly other supplies could be procured and delivered, contacting partners in the region to see if there were any leads on PPE in nearby countries.

Still, there was no way we were going to find a solution within twelve hours. It was the middle of the night in East Africa, and we would have to wait several hours before we even heard back from our partners in the region. Even if we were able to identify a contractor that might be able to expedite a procurement, the fastest delivery we could hope for would be in days, not hours.

I emailed Mark late that evening to let him know that I was not going to be able to deliver the PPE within Pete Marocco's twelve-hour deadline, but I wanted to let him know that I was trying, and that I hoped he wouldn't have to fire me.

"Keep trying," was all he wrote in response.

It was still February 19, still Mark's birthday. I felt an immense feeling of relief and vindication that I had refused to sing "Happy Birthday" to him earlier that day.

My team and I did keep trying. Most of that night, and the next several days as well, we explored every possible option. But there was no contractor that was able or willing to supply additional PPE on short notice without payment, which we could not guarantee. And there was no way to get the

PPE we had already paid for from the warehouse without an agreement with the WHO. On this, Pete Marocco refused to budge. While his underlings spared me from being fired for not transporting the PPE to Uganda within twelve hours, USAID failed to deliver the supplies needed for the outbreak response.

As far as I am aware, those twenty-seven thousand sets of PPE are still sitting in the WHO warehouse today, gathering dust and waiting to expire. All I know is, they never made it to Uganda.

18

Fool's Errand (Days 32–33)

The following day, Thursday, February 20, marked the one-month anniversary of Trump's inauguration. After a frustrating day of unsuccessful efforts to move PPE to Uganda to fight the Ebola outbreak, that was the night Natalia, Nida, Ramona, and I met at Astro Beer Hall after work. In the dark corner of the bar, we reflected in disbelief on how much ground we had lost in only thirty-one days. Tired and miserable, we debated where we should go from here. Our options were to continue our struggle within USAID to convince the political appointees of the value of our work in the hope of saving our programs, or to take a stand and forcefully speak out against the recklessness and cruelty of the administration's dismantling of the agency—to "blaze out," as Ramona put it.

By our third round of drinks, I had made up my mind. I was convinced that our best chance to save USAID was to expose publicly how the Trump administration was preventing us from implementing our lifesaving programs, and to lay bare the risks to public health and national security of shutting down the agency. I did not take this decision lightly. I knew it meant losing my job and likely the end of my career in civil service. But it was time to admit defeat. The dwindling hope that we might be able to save tiny fragments of our work was no longer worth the moral compromise we had been making by staying quiet about the administration's malfeasance.

We agreed that we would not go down quietly. In the memo that we would write and distribute, we'd document everything that had happened at USAID. Our hope was that our memo would one day serve to protect the USAID civil service workforce when the impact of the destruction became clear and the administration tried to put the blame on us.

As the top global health official at USAID, I had an opportunity to speak out from a platform that might make an impact. Maybe exposing what the administration was doing at USAID, from my position, would cause sufficient outrage to prompt Congress to step in and reverse the destruction. Or maybe no one would even care. But at least we would not be complicit in the destruction of the agency and our lifesaving work.

Leaving the bar that night, I felt a new sense of clarity. I knew what needed to be done. Now it was just a matter of compiling the documentation and then finding the right time to blaze out.

The next morning I walked into yet another manufactured crisis. State Department lawyers had repeatedly warned Pete Marocco that appropriations law required him to notify Congress before any irreversible steps were taken to close USAID, but he had ignored those warnings. Now, without a word of explanation, he decided that Congress needed to be notified immediately of the administration's plan to dismantle the agency.

At 8:30 a.m. he emailed Ken Jackson, Joel Borkert, Tim Meisburger, and Mark Lloyd, instructing them to submit the USAID closeout plan to him by ten o'clock in order for it to be submitted to Congress later that day. Mark forwarded the email to me at 9:12 a.m. and directed my team and teams from other bureaus to draft the congressional notification, which was due within the hour.

Around two dozen of us crowded into the basement conference room, speculating nervously about why we had only forty-five minutes to draft the notification to Congress. At the head of the table, Tim scribbled incomprehensibly across a whiteboard with a dry-erase marker. He scrawled shapes, arrows, and fictitious acronyms, betraying his unfamiliarity with USAID's structure in his rushed attempt to convey what he wanted us to do.

"We don't have much time," he blustered. "So here's what needs to happen. Take the few pieces of USAID that need to be moved over to State and show how they will fit in with the State org chart. It has to be quick, and it has to be clear."

As he spoke, Tim pointed at the whiteboard, from one indecipherable doodle to another, like a crazed battlefield general reviewing his ill-conceived attack plans. The silent room stared at him quizzically. After weeks of working group discussions to plan the "drawdown" of USAID, this was how we were going to articulate the plan to Congress?

Luckily, my team was prepared for this exercise. We had been brainstorming how GH's critical functions might be maintained even in the wake of USAID's demise. We assumed that Tim would be relieved to learn that we had already thought through the problem he was trying to solve.

Julie raised her hand to propose the solution we had devised. "There are several lifesaving global health programs that need to be continued," she began. "Those functions could be transferred over to State's Bureau of Global Health Security and Diplomacy—"

Tim cut her off immediately. "That's not gonna work," he said.

Julie blinked. "Sorry, I wasn't being clear," she said, trying again. "What I meant was, with some slight tweaks to their scope, they could take on several key functions—"

Again, Tim stopped her. "Still won't work," he said, shaking his head like a teacher dismissing an underperforming student.

"Why not?" Julie ventured.

"Because," Tim said, drawing out the word condescendingly, "we can't tell State bureaus what to do. We have to describe how USAID will bring its functions to State to do the work there. Then State can adjust their structures to align with us."

This made no sense to me. And from the skeptical stares around the room, I could see that my colleagues were equally baffled. It was true that the USAID staff in this meeting were poorly positioned to propose a re-organization at the State Department without the department's own staff present. But there was no time to bring them in.

Instead, Tim seemed to be suggesting that we should tell Congress that we wanted to effectively reconstitute USAID's functions at new bureaus to be created within the State Department. The idea seemed to completely ignore the political reality that there would be no appetite at the State Department for a plan, drawn up by outsiders, to set up these new bureaus. It was nonsense.

But without skipping a beat, Julie agreed with Tim. "Even better," she said, deploying the improv-comedy maxim "Yes, and . . ." like a seasoned performer. "We'll get to work drafting that up right away."

We now hurried to whip up a coherent proposal in the next thirty minutes. Natalia, Nida, Julie, Carmen Coles, Han Kang, and I began drafting a fantastical plan for what our hypothetical new State Department bureau would look like. I was busily transposing what we had already decided were GH's pared-down core functions—technical expertise on lifesaving disease programs, supply chain management, contract administration, international partnerships—when I stopped and took a look around.

The room was divided into three groups: global health, humanitarian assistance, and everyone else. Each group stood huddled around a laptop, desperately scrambling to incorporate their ideas into what we understood to be the official notification to Congress of what would remain of USAID's work. Tim had left the room, and several colleagues were frantically searching for him in the hope of receiving guidance on how to complete the task. Mark Lloyd reclined in a chair behind the GH group, arms crossed, intently observing our progress as if he were watching the Nature Channel from his living room sofa. No offer to help, no words of encouragement, no advice.

As my colleagues debated whether our imaginary new unit at State should be called the "Bureau *of* Lifesaving Assistance or the "Bureau *for* Lifesaving Assistance," I couldn't get past the absurdity. There would be no such bureau, whatever we wanted to call it. Maybe this was some kind of a test, or maybe the political appointees were in on the joke. Either way, it was clear that we were on a fool's errand, and I was done playing this demeaning game. Anger blurred the words on the screen until all I could see was my own rage.

Natalia, sitting next to me, noticed that I was glitching. She poked my shoulder.

"You okay?" she whispered.

"I'm done," I hissed through gritted teeth. I managed to meet her eyes. "Today is my last day."

"No!" she whispered back, a veteran long-distance runner coaxing me to finish the race. "We're not ready yet. You have to pull it together. Just keep writing—it won't be much longer."

The 10 a.m. deadline came and went—our time was up. Somehow, though we had been working on it for only half an hour, the GH plan was surprisingly coherent. But we had not had time to combine it with the other groups' work. And regardless of how everything meshed (or didn't) the result was wholly divorced from the State Department's structural realities.

At around ten fifteen, Tim reentered the room and informed us that the assignment was complete. He thanked us all, congratulating the group for pulling together on this important task on such short notice. Someone asked what the next steps would be before the congressional notification was sent to the Hill. Tim responded that he had sent USAID's plan to Pete Marocco a few minutes earlier, and it would be transmitted to Congress shortly.

Looks of surprise and confusion spread across the room.

"You already sent it?" Nida asked. "But we didn't even send you the document we were working on yet."

"That's all right," Tim said, as it finally dawned on the group that this entire exercise had been a sham. "It looked like you all were getting too deep into the weeds, so I just sent up a summary. Why don't you send me what you have now? We'll have to see, but maybe we can work it in later." Then he thanked us again and walked out.

Everyone quietly packed up and began shuffling out. I remained in my chair, frozen in humiliation and disgust. I stared straight ahead, unseeing, at my laptop screen, afraid of what I might do or say if I allowed myself to make eye contact with anyone at that moment.

Suddenly, I felt a heavy hand clamp down on my shoulder. I knew it was Mark Lloyd without looking up.

"Having fun yet?" he asked.

I kept staring at my screen. After a beat, he left, and I finally exhaled.

19.

A Catastrophic Approach (Days 34–37)

The week of February 24 was supposed to mark the beginning of a new normal, with the bare-bones "essential" employees (now officially notified of their continued employment) coming into the new USAID offices on 12th Street, and all others pushed to administrative leave, on the path to termination. Mark Lloyd had plans to meet with GH's "lifeboat crew" to introduce himself and formally kick off the final steady-state phase of USAID's remaining global health work.

But by Sunday evening, it was clear that for the foreseeable future we would still be mired in disorder and confusion. As expected, around five in the afternoon, I received an email informing me of my essential personnel status, my ticket to keep working at USAID. The message read: "You are receiving this message because you have been designated as essential personnel responsible for mission-critical functions, core leadership, and/or specially designated programs. This is your formal notification that you are expected to remain in working status, effective immediately and until notified otherwise." No surprise there, of course. I helped make the list.

Then, a couple hours later, another email came in, this one completely unexpected, and fully contradicting the previous one. Under the subject "Specific Notice of RIF," the email was a message from Pete Marocco, informing me that I was being fired: "I regret to inform you that you are affected by a Reduction in Force (RIF) action. This RIF is necessary to restructure USAID's operations to better reflect Agency priorities and the foreign policy priorities of the United States. . . . Consequently, you will be separated from the Federal service effective April 24, 2025."

This one threw me. I had been preparing to come in the next morning under my new essential status. I wasn't exactly looking forward to what the future looked like for USAID, but at least I had been told I had a place in it. And then, out of the blue, a Sunday night email from a senior Trump appointee was informing me that my position was being eliminated, and I was being fired.

I quickly learned that I was not the only one to receive the conflicting messages—first one confirming that we were critically important for the agency's mission, and then another that our positions were being eliminated because they did not align with agency priorities. While the political appointees had worked all the previous week to identify a small group to carry out USAID's core functions, DOGE had found a way to slash entire categories of staff without needing to identify a reason. The problem, though, was that these lists did not match. In GH, approximately a quarter of the designated essential staff also received RIF notifications that night. In a clear sign that no one had compared the lists before sending them out, Mark Lloyd himself received a RIF notification email. He was as baffled as the rest of us, responding to our confused inquiries that he assumed there must have been a mistake and he would try to get it sorted out in the morning.

And so on Monday morning, I went to the 12th Street office early. For the first time, we were no longer relegated to the Programs Group conference room in the basement; there were now actual workstations reserved for GH. I surveyed the area that was assigned to our remaining team. Unlike the Reagan Building, where the cubicles and offices were left untouched, our new workspace on the ninth floor, which had been previously occupied by the Bureau for Humanitarian Assistance, had been wiped clean. No trace remained of the teams that, until recently, had been responsible for the U.S. government's response to famines, natural disasters, and other humanitarian crises around the world. The spotless desks appeared as if they had never been used. Everything looked clean and new. Someone had taken painstaking efforts to make the space look like a suitable setting for a fresh start. If only the immaculate facade hadn't been spoiled by the termination letters we had received the night before.

Julie arrived before me that morning, ready to forge a new path for global health with what she, too, was now calling the "lifeboat crew." She had chosen for herself the office closest to where the political appointees sat and then offered me the next pick. But closing myself off from my colleagues during this period of uncertainty did not feel right. Instead, I found a table in the center of the open GH space and decided to set up my laptop there. We were going to have approximately sixty employees arriving that day, coming into the new office for the first time. There would be many questions, and I wanted to make myself available, even though I knew I would have few answers.

That morning, as Ramona, Nida, and I served as a welcoming committee, Julie and Natalia met with Mark and Tim for the fruitless daily update on the status of our lifesaving programs. When they returned from the meeting, they caught my attention, looking perturbed.

"We have a problem," Julie told me. "Tim just told us that he's not going to approve the Ebola response as a lifesaving activity."

"How is that possible?" I asked.

I wasn't surprised that the political appointees were refusing to lift a finger to restart the activities to support Uganda in response to the outbreak. This had been going on for weeks. But their justification had always been framed in terms of the difficulties navigating the broken payment system. This was the first time they had said out loud that they did not even consider Ebola prevention to be lifesaving.

"How are they rationalizing that combating an outbreak of a virus with one of the world's highest mortality rates is not lifesaving?" I continued.

"I just don't think they trust us," Julie responded. "Only two deaths have been reported in this outbreak, and they think we're overstating the risk as a way to restart non-lifesaving work. They think the outbreak is already under control. The bottom line is, we need to stop pushing on the Ebola response activities."

I wanted to argue. Julie and I had just met, once again, with the Outbreak Response Team, who had briefed us on the protocol for an Ebola outbreak. The virus has an incubation period of up to twenty-one days, and it is crucial to stay vigilant during that period in case infections spread undetected. We were still within the twenty-one-day window, and it was not yet time to declare the outbreak over. If it turned out that new cases were detected while we did nothing, our response would be even further behind.

But Julie cut me off. "We need to be strategic," she said. "We're not going to convince them. Let's focus our energy on the activities that Mark and Tim agree are lifesaving."

When she walked away, Natalia pulled me aside, her eyes wide with shock and fury, and I had a feeling that Julie had not told me the whole story. "It's impossible to reason with them," Natalia whispered to me. "Tim told us that 'Ebola is a scam.' He called it a scam! This is not how public health works!"

Natalia was right, there was no reasoning with someone who refused to acknowledge the threat of a deadly infectious disease. We were accustomed to debating cost-effectiveness and comparative advantage to ensure our approach was as impactful as possible, but we were simply unprepared to persuade political appointees that the Ebola outbreak was indeed a real threat that warranted a response.

I soon learned that Tim was not the only political appointee willing to suspend reality when it came to the Ebola outbreak. The National Security Council was growing increasingly concerned about USAID's lack of response to the outbreak in Uganda, as well as the concurrent Marburg outbreak in Tanzania. Later that day, the NSC senior director for biosecurity and pandemic response policy emailed Pete Marocco with his concerns:

> Suspended access to the USAID Phoenix Financial System is impeding direct implementation of outbreak response activities in the midst of two viral hemorrhagic fever outbreaks. . . . We are also hearing that "Reduction In Force" notices have been issued to grant agreement offi-

cers and health officers who cover or are stationed on the continent of Africa. Again, where two active viral hemorrhagic fever outbreaks put several countries in East and Central Africa at risk of spread without sufficient staff in place to continue ongoing mission critical activities. . . . I would like to take the opportunity to request an urgent meeting with you and your team to better understand what has actually happened, and if you agree, to offer my perspective from the national security biothreat landscape that may warrant calibrated adjustment of the RIF process to maintain mission critical personnel needed to support ongoing viral hemorrhagic fever outbreaks.

In his reply, Marocco lied about the status of USAID's Ebola response, while downplaying the threat. Although none of the Ebola response activities had been approved, he wrote: "We have approved every Ebola support program I am aware of—even the ones that we believe may have exaggerated magnitude." While it is possible that he was unaware that Tim, Mark, and Ken Jackson were holding up several Ebola response activities at their level, there were other Ebola activities that Marocco had personally vetoed. I knew firsthand, for example, that he was directly responsible for refusing to authorize the delivery of PPE to Uganda from the WHO warehouse in Kenya.

That afternoon, Carmen Coles and I met with Mark to try to nail down which activities he would consider approving as lifesaving and which he would not. We printed our spreadsheet of all the activities that we were requesting, none of which had been approved to date, and brought it to the meeting, prepared to explain why each activity on our list was necessary to avert imminent loss of life.

Mark's message was clear. "Trim the fat," he told us. "We're looking at each activity very closely, and we're not going to consider anything that isn't really saving lives, like now."

But we had already heard this line from him several times. I reminded Mark that we had gone back to the program managers for each of these activities, and they had spent hours with the technical experts, painstakingly pinpointing the specific number of lives that would be saved by each proposed intervention. There was no more fat to trim. Cutting any further would be guaranteed to cost lives. He snapped on his glasses, took our spreadsheet, and one by one, as his eyes skimmed over the paragraphs of justification we had prepared, drew an *X* through most of the activities with his pencil to mark his disapproval. Then he handed it back.

"Okay, I'll be very direct," he said, sighing. "We're not going to approve activities for bird flu, or Ebola, or polio, or monkeypox, or the neglected tropical diseases. They aren't killing anyone right now. And don't go telling me that one lady died of bird flu in Kansas, so now the whole thing is life-saving. That's not going to fly. And another thing: Get rid of the activities you have on this list that are for things like monitoring or surveillance. If you can't show me the actual person who is going to die if we don't do the activity, then we're not doing it."

I tried to explain that his parameters were flawed and would cost lives. If we couldn't conduct surveillance or monitoring activities, how would we be able to respond to future outbreaks? Ignoring infectious diseases like bird flu until significant clusters of human deaths were reported was a catastrophic approach. For polio and some of our neglected tropical disease programs, we were on the brink of eliminating terrible diseases that had scourged humanity for centuries. To take our foot off the gas pedal now would jeopardize all the progress we had made. And, of course, Ebola was killing people. Just because only two deaths had been reported from the current outbreak so far did not mean that responding to the outbreak was not a lifesaving activity. But, despite his lack of expertise or experience in the health field, Mark could not be convinced. He was done listening to global health experts.

Back in the GH space on the other side of the floor, I regrouped with my team and broke the news of the new, inadequate definition of "lifesaving" we were now limited to. I saw the pain in the eyes of our infectious disease experts as they realized that I had failed to convince Mark that people would die without these activities. At the same time, there were still activities on our spreadsheet that Mark hadn't crossed out, primarily for

TB, malaria, and HIV, along with nutrition programs and maternal and child health efforts. These still had a chance of being approved. We needed to get a pared-down list back to Mark right away.

But Mark's directive presented a moral quandary: Should we cut the activities he had marked, knowing that this would cost lives, in order to push forward the remaining programs, or should we refuse to cut any lifesaving activities, even if that put all our work at risk?

The dilemma came to a head over the Ebola response. Mark had asked us to remove our three requests related to the outbreak: to support community health workers to conduct contact tracing; to implement infection control measures to prevent the disease from spreading; and to provide treatment services to the sick. Julie now made the point that we needed to follow the direction of our political appointee. The Ebola plan was not going to be approved; keeping it on the list would only serve to hurt our relationship with Mark, and thus our credibility to influence him on the other activities. Nida, along with the Outbreak Response Team, forcefully disagreed, arguing that it was our duty as global health officials to continue to push for an activity that we knew was needed, even if it was ultimately rejected.

I was not sure what to do. I wanted to keep advocating for the Ebola activities. Removing them would be bowing to political pressure to take an unjustifiable position, especially in light of the secretary of state's waiver for lifesaving assistance. On the other hand, Julie was correct on a practical level; the activities wouldn't be approved no matter what I did. And if there was a chance for TB patients to resume their treatment, for ambulance services to be restarted for emergency childbirths, for bed nets to be distributed in malaria-prone regions, didn't I need to prioritize those activities over the ill-fated Ebola response? I decided that I did, and I struck the Ebola activities from our list. Nida did not have to voice her disappointment with my decision. The death stare she gave me told me everything I needed to know.

The next day, we received a report that two additional people had died from Ebola in Uganda, including a four-year-old boy. The concerns of the

Outbreak Response Team had been realized; the outbreak was not over, nor was it a scam. As soon as I learned this, I restored to our spreadsheet the Ebola activities I had removed the previous day.

Nothing had been approved since I had sent the list to Mark; those lives would not have been saved if I hadn't removed the activities. Yet I was ashamed by the choice I had made. I had abandoned the evidence-based decision-making on which USAID had always prided itself. I had followed what I believed was an illegitimate order from a political appointee, one with potentially deadly consequences, rather than stand up for what I knew was right. I promised myself I would not do this again.

20.

Millions of Lives (Day 38)

On Wednesday, February 26, I was leading a meeting for the GH Bureau's remaining staff when the malaria team received an email that derailed the discussion. In a quiet voice that shook with distress, the malaria director told us that the primary contractor responsible for USAID's malaria drugs and supplies was reporting that its contract had just been terminated.

While this was not the first time we had found out from our implementers that their contracts had been terminated without any advance notice from USAID, this was by far the most consequential. This was our flagship malaria contract, essential to continue lifesaving drugs and services that protected millions of people from this deadly disease, one of the world's top killers of children under five. USAID's malaria program was entirely dependent on the continuation of this contract. "This means the end of our malaria program," said the director.

"It's gotta be a mistake," the program manager for the contract said. "I bet I know what happened. The malaria contract number is only one off from the contract number for our family planning contract. They must have been trying to terminate that one, and accidentally got the contract number wrong. There's no way they meant to cut off all malaria drugs right before the rainy season. We just need them to correct the mistake."

"I hope you're right," I said. "But at this point, I'm not assuming anything is a mistake. I'll try to find out what happened, but please start drafting a note for me to warn them—in the simplest possible terms—how bad it will be if this contract is terminated. I'm going to need an exact estimate of how many lives will be lost in the short term without it."

I quickly sent a message to Jami Rodgers and Nadeem Shah in our contracting office, warning them that the malaria contract had just been terminated, but it was needed under the lifesaving waiver. Without it, millions of lives would be imminently at risk. When I didn't immediately hear back, I left the conference room, with the malaria team trailing at my heels, to go looking for Jami or Nadeem.

They were not in their offices. Even as I clung to the hope that there had been a mistake, I continued my search for them, knowing that there was no higher priority for global health at that moment than whatever chance we had of rescinding the effective termination of our malaria program. But before I could find them, I learned that the situation was even worse than I had feared.

The head of the tuberculosis team caught up to me as I continued my laps around the building. She had just received an email from the partner who implemented our flagship TB contract, responsible for nearly all drugs and diagnostics. It, too, had been terminated, signifying the end of USAID's TB program. Tuberculosis is the world's leading infectious disease killer, and its increasingly shifty drug-resistant strains pose a foreseeable health risk—not just in developing countries but in America as well.

Within the hour, I heard the same story from our maternal and child health team. Their flagship contract had also received a letter of termination that afternoon. I learned that all three letters were identical, each addressed to "Dear Implementing Partner" with only the contract number to distinguish one letter from the next. They all stated: "This award is being terminated for convenience and the interests of the U.S. Government. . . . Secretary Rubio and . . . Deputy Administrator Marocco have determined your award is not aligned with Agency priorities and made a determination that continuing this program is not in the national interest." Each letter was signed by Nadeem Shah.

Finally, I caught up to Nadeem outside a conference room, where he was about to enter a meeting. By now, I had a sizable entourage in tow:

most of the malaria team as well as some people from the TB and maternal and child health teams. What else did they have to do? The entire future of their programs rested on whether or not these contracts were terminated.

Normally thoughtful, soft-spoken, and meticulously organized, Nadeem was well regarded as a practical and solutions-oriented procurement official with a calming, warm smile. But that afternoon he looked totally flustered and disheveled, as if he had just finished running a particularly grueling race. When I made eye contact, he appeared to be neither happy nor surprised to see me. I could only imagine the pressure he must have been under at that moment, having terminated an unknown number of lifesaving contracts that day.

But I did not have time for pleasantries. "You sent termination letters to our most critical contracts," I said, jumping right in. "Without the contracts you terminated today, our malaria, TB, and maternal and child health programs won't be able to function. This will cost the lives of millions. You promised to let me review GH contracts before they were terminated to make sure you weren't ending lifesaving programs, but today you ended our most important lifesaving programs without even a warning!"

"I'm sorry, Nick," Nadeem said softly, sounding truly apologetic. "We got the list this morning and were told there would be no exceptions. There were thousands of contracts on the list. We weren't even allowed to send the list to contracting officers. There was no time for a review. I had to process all the terminations myself."

"How could you sign them?" I demanded. And when he didn't answer me, I asked again: "How could you do it? The malaria contract alone was providing lifesaving services to fifty-four million people. How could you sign a letter terminating that contract?"

"I didn't have a choice," he said. He offered to talk further later that afternoon and then hustled off to his meeting. Once he left, I felt bad for confronting him like that. Had I not made a similarly bad choice, albeit on a far smaller scale, the previous day? He was doubtless under pressure that I did not understand. Still, he did have a choice. He could have chosen not to sign those letters. Maybe the contracts would have been terminated by someone else instead, but at least those letters would not have his signature on them.

As Nadeem had said, those three critical contracts were not the only ones terminated that day. February 26 marked the functional end of almost all USAID's global health programming. Nearly every GH contract received a termination letter, including the ones needed to provide lifesaving services for HIV, polio, neglected tropical diseases, family planning, emerging infectious diseases, and nutrition. At the time, we had no way of knowing which contracts had been terminated. Only Nadeem, Jami, DOGE, and the political appointees had seen the full list, and they refused to share it. So the bad news continued to trickle in all afternoon as we learned of each termination individually, only when a program manager received a communication from a contractor notifying us that its contract had been terminated.

The timing of the mass terminations was no coincidence. It was a calculated response intended to subvert a court order, which Jeremy Lewin had announced the previous week when he told the Coordination Support Team that he would rather terminate USAID's contracts than pay the agency's outstanding debts. Nearly two weeks after a federal judge ordered USAID to pay the contractors for their previously incurred costs, the agency had done nothing to release the funds. The judge evidently grew impatient with the administration's stalling, because on February 25 he issued a new order, this time with a deadline for the outstanding costs to be paid by midnight on February 26. With the deadline looming, Jeremy followed through on his threat to terminate the contracts rather than comply with the court's ruling.

That same afternoon, Elon Musk was back in the White House, this time at a cabinet meeting, where on live TV he told Trump and all his top advisors with a chuckle that: "One of the things that we accidentally canceled, very briefly, was Ebola prevention. I think we all want Ebola prevention. So we restored the Ebola prevention immediately, and there was no interruption."

Of course, this was no more true this time than it had been when he said the same thing two weeks earlier. If anything, it was more outrageous. In reality, at the same time that Musk was publicly lying about restoring Ebola prevention activities, the contracts that were needed to implement those activities were being terminated on the grounds that the work was "not in the national interest."

It was not just Musk who was lying. The mass contract terminations on February 26 finally revealed that Rubio's waiver allowing lifesaving humanitarian assistance had been a farce. Admittedly, I'd had my doubts all along, but I'd kept pushing in case even some services could be even partially restored. So much for all our efforts over the past month to justify which activities were needed to save lives, to beg for them to be approved. So much for our attempts to fix the broken payment system to allow contractors to continue their work. So much for the daily Programs Group meetings to troubleshoot the challenges for implementing USAID's lifesaving work. A single mail-merged termination letter, copied to thousands of contractors, had rendered moot everything we had done to try to save our most critical programs.

In hindsight this looks naive, but I was still not ready to give up. I called Julie, who was out of the office that day attending to a family matter, and broke the news to her. I told her that I was going to appeal the terminations immediately, raising my concerns to Joel Borkert, Ken Jackson, Pete Marocco, as far up the chain as I could go. She urged restraint, imploring me to take my concerns to Mark instead. "If you go over his head," she warned, "he will think you're trying to make him look bad. This is not over, but we need to work through Mark on this. Remember, our job is to be helpful to him."

The idea of staying in our lane as USAID's entire global health portfolio collapsed around us seemed foolhardy. I wondered if I had not adequately conveyed how desperate the situation had become, so I decided to drop my normal professionalism in favor of bluntness.

"Mark won't do shit," I shouted. "Isn't that obvious by now? All this time, we've tried to raise everything up through Mark, always being careful to not go over his head. And where has that gotten us? Nowhere. We don't have time to waste going back and forth with Mark today. We need to elevate these contract terminations to someone who might be able to do something about them before it's too late—if it isn't already."

I returned to Nadeem's office later that afternoon and found him staring nervously at the list of contracts that had just been terminated. After apologizing for calling him out earlier in front of so many colleagues, I told him I had come to see if there was any way that the terminations could be reversed, at least for those contracts that were needed for lifesaving activities. Nadeem said that some rescissions may be possible, and may, in fact, be necessary.

Several of the terminated contracts, he told me, had turned out to be necessary to provide basic safety, security, and operational capacity services for the agency. The contract that provided phone plans for all USAID employees had been terminated, for example. So had the lease for the building we had just moved into on 12th Street. In another irony, one of the terminations was the contract for the agency's system that managed the termination of contracts. Other terminations included contracts that provided critical infrastructure to keep American staff overseas safe and, in some cases, alive. Nadeem had received a panicked call from the USAID mission in South Sudan, where the contract that provides potable water to the staff there had been terminated, leading to the immediate rationing of the suddenly limited supply of drinking water.

"They made a lot of obvious mistakes," Nadeem told me. "And now we're scrambling to see which of those we can fix."

I asked him to add to his list of mistakes those contracts that had been terminated that were providing lifesaving humanitarian assistance pursuant to Rubio's waiver. In addition to the examples I had already shared with him for malaria, Ebola, TB, and maternal and child health, the list continued to grow by the hour. By now, my team had begun to hear from overseas missions as well, and our incomplete count was already up to nearly two hundred contracts with lifesaving activities that had been terminated that day, including more than one hundred HIV programs in various countries that cumulatively provided lifesaving HIV treatment to 5 million people. "If we can't get these terminations rescinded," I told him, "we're looking at loss of life on an unimaginable scale."

I asked Nadeem how the terminated contracts had been selected. He said there was no clear pattern. The list he had received from Jeremy Lewin included contracts large and small, from all countries, operational and programmatic, working in all sectors. Jeremy had told him that the list had been vetted and approved by Rubio, but it was unclear how that vetting process had operated.

Nadeem's best guess was that someone had conducted a keyword search of the list of contract titles to identify essential contracts that should not be terminated. But, as anyone who has participated in the process of naming government contracts could attest, it was impossible to glean the purpose of a contract solely from its title. USAID contract titles usually were cringeworthy acronyms thought up by nerdy bureaucrats. (I immediately thought of the ENDOR contract—Ending Neglected Diseases through Operational Research—and wondered how the DOGE team had determined whether or not to terminate the contract which had been named by a *Star Wars*–obsessed infectious disease specialist after the fictional home planet of the adorable Ewoks in *Return of the Jedi*.) Of the dozens of contracts I had managed in my career, I can't think of a single one whose purpose could be identified solely by reading its name.

Jeremy's process to identify which critical contracts should not be terminated—a decision with life-and-death consequences—had been doomed to fail from the start. His approach had been no more strategic than if he had asked a toddler to look at the list of USAID contracts and point to the ones we should keep. If he had checked with anyone with experience working on USAID contracts, he would have immediately learned that his "vetting process" would not work. Each of the numerous mistakes that were now popping up was another indication that neither Jeremy nor anyone else in the Trump administration cared which contracts were terminated and which were saved.

I was no longer surprised by the extent of the administration's careless disregard for the impact of its decisions. But Nadeem's description of the chaos that was unfolding gave me hope that there might still be a window to mitigate the damage before it was too late. Even if it was a long shot, I needed to try to get some of the termination letters rescinded.

Late that afternoon, I met with my GH team again. With nearly all the contracts needed to implement lifesaving programs terminated, this was no time for optimism, and I felt I owed it to my colleagues to be honest and realistic about the situation. I had nothing to hide, so I did not even bother finding a conference room. Instead, we met at the table I had commandeered in the middle of the GH open space, where any of the political appointees could walk by at any minute. Many of my colleagues were in tears, or on the brink. For those who had started the week newly designated as essential employees, they had returned to work with a degree of confidence that their jobs were safe and their programs had been deemed important. But now, without any warning, everything they had been working on had been ripped away in an instant. It seemed like the end.

I did not want to give any more false hope. I wanted to be clear exactly how dire the situation was. I told my assembled colleagues that I had not given up and that there still might be a fleeting chance to reverse some of the most critical terminations. But the reality was that USAID was being shuttered, and, despite all our efforts these past weeks, we had been prevented from implementing our lifesaving work at every turn. I could not, in good conscience, continue to tell them that implementing the waiver was our top priority.

From this point forward, I said, our top priority was to bear witness to the destruction and to document every attempt we had made to save lives, the administrative stonewalling we'd run into, and all our pleas and warnings of the damage being done by the reckless dismantling of our agency. I told them that we needed the documentation to protect us, that we owed it to our former colleagues who had already been purged, and that the world one day would need to know what happened here.

The time had come to write one last memo.

21.

A New Purpose (Day 39)

There was a new camaraderie among the Bureau for Global Health's remaining staff starting on Thursday, February 27. Gallows humor prevailed. People brought in donuts and pastries, leaving them on my table in the center of our work area, which had become a cathartic, informal gathering space. Someone posted a facetious label on the pastry boxes: LIFESAVING HUMANITARIAN ASSISTANCE. Ramona set up her friendship bracelet kit at the table, and several colleagues beaded witty messages for one another: ESSENTIALLY RIFFED (a tribute to our amorphous and contradictory employment status); SEND ME A SIGNAL (referring to the encrypted messaging app Signal, which was quickly becoming the favorite communication tool among USAID staff fearing surveillance and retribution from the administration); WHAT THE FORK? (a reference to Elon Musk's dubious ultimatum for employees across the federal government to voluntarily resign, in an email titled "Fork in the Road").

With the abrupt termination of our contracts the previous day, a sense of resignation had begun to set in. Until then, we had believed we might be able to reverse the terminations of our lifesaving programs, and we had continued to compile lists of contracts that had been terminated, making the case to Mark, Tim, and Joel to rescind the terminations. But now any sense of optimism had vanished. The more I pushed USAID's political appointees, the clearer it became that they were simply annoyed that I kept pointing out their mistakes in terminating our critical contracts. "Take a step back," Mark chastised me by email, in response to my continued warnings that the terminations would cumulatively cost millions of lives.

At Thursday's Programs Group meeting, the termination of nearly all USAID contracts was, unsurprisingly, the top agenda item for the group tasked with ensuring the implementation of the lifesaving humanitarian assistance waiver. When we pointed out that most of the contracts needed to implement lifesaving activities had been terminated, Tim Meisburger brazenly shifted the blame for this mistake to the career staff.

"The problem is, the names of all those contracts were unclear," he said accusingly. "There's no way to tell if they were lifesaving or not, it's all just a jumble of alphabet soup. It was impossible to see which contracts were lifesaving and which weren't."

Nida did not let him get away with that. "That's because when we named them, we didn't realize those names would be used as the basis for deciding whether or not they would be terminated," she responded.

This was the second time I had heard from our agency's leadership that the decisions for contract terminations had been made based solely on a contract's name, and I was no less dismayed. If they didn't know what the contracts did, they could have asked. Instead, they had terminated them all.

Ironically, that same day the Office of Management and Budget issued guidance on how the administration would conduct the foreign assistance review mandated in Trump's executive order pausing foreign assistance. The EO had conditioned the ninety-day foreign assistance pause "pending reviews of such programs for programmatic efficiency and consistency with United States foreign policy." It specified that the administration "will make determinations within 90 days of this order on whether to continue, modify, or cease each foreign assistance program based upon the review recommendations." Now, on February 27, even though USAID's political leadership had already effectively terminated nearly all foreign assistance programs, OMB had defined the review process.

The timing of the new guidance, coming the day after the mass terminations, was disorienting. The administration had sent an unequivocal signal that the results of the review were predetermined. As the initial step in the foreign assistance review process, the guidance directed contractors to evaluate their own programs for alignment with the "America First" foreign policy platform. However, the vast majority of contractors had just received a letter informing them that their contracts had been terminated because they were "not aligned with the Agency's priorities" and "not in the national interest."

At the Programs Group meeting, I asked Tim about the contradiction between the OMB guidance, which suggested that the review of our programs was still to come, and the termination letters, which suggested that the matter had already been settled. He dismissed my concern with a disgusted flip of his hand.

Amid the confusion, Julie came up with a new plan to persuade the political appointees to rescind the terminations of some of our most critical contracts. Her idea was to use the foreign assistance review process to negotiate with our political leaders by offering contracts that had not yet been terminated to be sacrificed in exchange for reinstating some of the terminated contracts.

Even though we were desperate to find a way to rescind the terminations, for me Julie's idea was a nonstarter. It would mean affirmatively recommending the termination of some of our global health contracts, which I believed was neither legal nor technically advisable. Indeed, these were programs that we had created in the first place, and there was no justification to recommend their termination. There was no basis in federal procurement law, much less global health policy, to barter the viability of one of our contracts in exchange for saving another.

Worse still, if career USAID officials were to put forth recommendations for the termination of some of our few remaining contracts, I surmised that the political appointees might use those recommendations to justify further cuts. In my calculus, the risk of losing more contracts, as well as the risk of providing cover to political appointees trying to justify the terminations, dwarfed the hope that Julie's strategy would result in any contracts being reinstated.

Even as the hopelessness of our situation settled in, our one remaining task—documenting our agency's destruction—instilled a new feeling of purpose among the GH team. Rumors began to spread that employees who had received RIF letters despite their designation as essential employees might be imminently placed on administrative leave. This included me, as well as the rest of the dwindling GH leadership group. We established a continuity plan, designating successors to take on various functions in case our positions were suddenly eliminated. We identified the director of HIV as the logical assistant administrator designee, and began including her in all senior-level discussions and engagements with the political appointees as a way to ease the anticipated transition.

Furthermore, I started to detect hints in the tone of emails and discussions that the political appointees were ready to be rid of me specifically. In addition to the "take a step back" email, Mark was furious with me for continuing to raise the contract-termination issue with Joel and Ken. And in my interactions with Tim at the Programs Group meeting I perceived his increasing disgust with me and my team. If I was going to compile and release the memos before being kicked out, we needed to move quickly.

We didn't have much time, but our task would not take long. Whatever else we had faced over the past weeks, we were still good bureaucrats, and we knew how to write a memo. The work was split into three categories: how we had been prevented from implementing lifesaving activities despite Rubio's waiver; the decimation of the GH workforce; and the impact of the destruction of USAID's global health projects. As acting assistant administrator for global health, I would be named as the author of the memos, and it would fall to me to send them, but drafting them was a full team effort and a welcome new focus for the GH staff, who had found themselves without any active programs to manage.

My plan was to email the memos to the nearly eight hundred staff members who had worked in GH prior to January 20. I wanted to ensure that they had access to the memos for their records, so they would be able to specifically document their efforts to preserve our work and warn the administration of the dire impacts of slashing GH's programs. However, because most of these eight hundred individuals either had been fired or were on administrative leave, I decided to send the memos to their personal email addresses—which we had collected for emergency preparedness purposes—in addition to their USAID accounts, many of which were no longer active.

While my primary focus was to ensure that the GH staff had the memos for their personal records, I was confident that an added benefit of sharing the memos so broadly was that they would quickly make their way to the press and then into public view. The American people, and others around the world, needed to read the assessment by USAID's top global health official of what the Trump administration had done to the agency, and the impact of the destruction. I felt driven to set the record straight about exactly who and what was responsible for recklessly shuttering USAID, and I believed that an objective account of the facts was crucial to eventually hold the administration accountable for its actions.

Ramona drafted the first memo, titled "Documentation of Challenges and Impediments to Implementing the Lifesaving Humanitarian Assistance Waiver for the Pause on Foreign Assistance (Jan 28–Feb 28)." She meticulously recounted every effort we had made to restart our frozen global health programs, starting from the issuance of Rubio's waiver on January 28. She and her team pored through thousands of pages of emails, notes, and records to present a comprehensive timeline of all our requests, pleas, and warnings about the need to restart our programs in order to save lives. The seven-page, single-spaced memo documented in detail how we had been thwarted at every turn by DOGE and our political leadership, from shutting down our payment system to repeatedly issuing contradictory guidance, to indefensibly narrowing the definition of "lifesaving," to ultimately terminating all the contracts needed to implement lifesaving activities. The memo concluded:

> Successful implementation of Secretary Rubio's temporary waiver to the pause on foreign assistance for lifesaving humanitarian assistance

was not possible due to administrative and bureaucratic challenges, including contradictory and shifting guidance regarding approval for required activities and failure of Agency leadership to process disbursement of funds for activities once approved. As a result of these challenges, the Bureau for Global Health (GH) has been wholly prevented from delivering lifesaving activities under the waiver to date. . . .

USAID's failure to implement lifesaving humanitarian assistance under the waiver is the result of political leadership at USAID, the Department of State, and DOGE, who have created and continue to create intentional and/or unintentional obstacles that have wholly prevented implementation. . . . These actions individually and in combination have resulted in the U.S. Government's failure to implement critical lifesaving activities. This will no doubt result in preventable death, destabilization, and threats to national security on a massive scale.

Natalia wrote the second memo, titled "Documentation of Bureau for Global Health Workforce Reductions," which was intended to be read in tandem with Ramona's memo. Natalia focused on the reckless and debilitating cuts to our staffing footprint, starting with the first terminations in January and the temporary severance of our bureau leadership, and then tracking the progressive firings, seesawing administrative leave, and RIF letters that wrecked our operational capacity throughout February, up to our current meager roster of fewer than 10 percent of the staff we had employed a month earlier. The memo documented how the "drastic staffing reductions have severely impacted GH's ability to function."

More than this, Natalia's memo memorialized how the cuts affected each of the 783 individual staff members who had worked in the Bureau for Global Health on January 20. The cuts instituted by DOGE and the political appointees were as clumsy and impersonal as a chainsaw and demonstrated a gross indifference to the individuals affected. As she wrote the memo, Natalia and her team struggled to respond to dozens of fraught requests from abandoned staff members who were trying to figure out whether they still had jobs, whether they were about to lose their health insurance, or were merely in search of documentation of their termination so they could apply for unemployment benefits. So-called probationary employees—individuals who had not yet served long enough to meet the minimum requirements for civil service protections (usually two years)—were fired, then reinstated by court orders, only to be fired again. Other GH employees who were on the essential staffing list were still unable to access their email, remaining in limbo long after they had been deemed essential to return to work. Natalia captured the plight of many of these individuals who had been cast aside by the imprecise and sloppy drawdown of USAID.

The third memo, "Risks to U.S. National Security and Public Health: Consequences of Pausing Global Health Funding for Lifesaving Humanitarian Assistance," was our official warning to the administration of the impact of halting critical global health programs. The drafting process was led by GH's chief data scientist, who worked with each of our health teams to estimate the real-world consequences of abruptly freezing our lifesaving work. This memo presented modeling compiled across each of USAID's global health programs and documented how the cuts to our programs "will lead to increased death and disability, accelerate global disease spread, contribute to destabilizing fragile regions, and heightened security risks—directly endangering American national security, economic stability, and public health." Until now, our prior warnings had specified the risks of failing to restart an individual activity or failing to respond to a particular outbreak. Now we compiled the risks across all our frozen programs, and the cumulative devastation was overwhelming.

Overall, the modeling and analysis concluded that a staggering 2.6 million additional people would die per year due to the cuts to USAID's global health programs. Broken down by individual disease program, the cuts would result in a 39 percent annual increase in malaria cases, and as many as 166,000 additional malaria deaths; a 30 percent annual increase in tuberculosis (including drug-resistant strains) globally; as many as 28,000 additional cases of viral hemorrhagic fever, like Ebola or Marburg; and an additional 200,000 annual cases of paralytic polio, along with hundreds of millions of new polio infections overall.

Furthermore, our estimates showed that the cessation of USAID's global health activities would result annually in 16.8 million pregnant women not receiving services like essential medications and services for postpartum hemorrhaging and eclampsia; 11.2 million newborn babies not receiving critical postnatal care within two days of childbirth; 14.8 million children not receiving treatment for pneumonia and diarrhea, two of the top causes of preventable death in children under age five; more than 3 million people with HIV losing access to their lifesaving treatment; and 1 million children not treated for severe acute malnutrition.

Beyond the risks to lives around the world, the memo documented the substantial risks to U.S. national security, including how the halt to global health programs increases the risk of dangerous diseases reaching the United States. In a globally connected world, outbreaks abroad do not stay overseas. The memo described how the chances of U.S. exposure to infectious diseases through travel, the movement of military personnel, and migration rise when public health systems fail to contain outbreaks at their source, and how uncontrolled epidemics abroad could trigger serious outbreaks in America.

The memo warned that without effective disease surveillance networks, the U.S. would be flying blind until diseases show up at our own border, a recipe for more imported outbreaks on American soil. We gave the example of the 2014 Ebola outbreak in West Africa, where the detection and containment of the outbreak prevented it from becoming a larger crisis. Even so, the few Ebola cases that did reach the U.S. at that time illustrated the heavy burden of managing dangerous contagions: A single Ebola patient in New York had cost the city health department $4.3 million in response measures. If global surveillance and response capacity erode, the U.S. could face multiple such cases or simultaneous outbreaks, which could overwhelm American hospitals and our public health system, a direct threat to our national security. Overseas, the deterioration of fragile health systems worsens migration and conflict, creating ideal conditions for the spread of extremism and for recruitment by terrorist groups.

Finally, the memo warned that the halting of USAID's global health activities posed substantial risks to U.S. foreign policy interests, including economic impacts on U.S. trade and markets. It described how heightened disease burdens caused by the cuts would reduce productivity in key regions. Diseases like malaria, HIV, and TB primarily strike working-age adults or their children, impairing productivity and economic output in Africa, Asia, and beyond. Malaria alone costs African economies an estimated $12 billion per year in lost GDP from worker absenteeism, lower productivity, and healthcare expenses. The memo described how unchecked high rates of maternal and childhood morbidity or mortality can exacerbate impacts on productivity, and how increased malnutrition can reduce a nation's GDP by as much as 16.5 percent. (Malnourished children perform worse in school, and this translates into productivity losses as adults.) Lower productivity in these regions weakens their economic output and trade capacity, thereby diminishing their ability to import U.S. goods and services. Over the long term, this undermines global economic growth.

My intention was for the memos to expose the lies, ineptitude, indifference, and callousness of DOGE and the political appointees, who had prevented us from implementing lifesaving programs during the first weeks of the Trump administration—and the catastrophic impact on human lives around the world that was likely to result from their actions. But it was critical that the memos adhere exclusively to hard facts. My concern was that, when the memos became public, the administration would attempt to tarnish my reputation as a nonpartisan global health expert, and instead try to paint me as a disgruntled partisan hack—an actor of the "deep state"—insubordinately refusing to implement the new administration's policies.

The only way I could think to combat that perception was to limit the memos' content strictly to a recitation of the specific actions we had taken to implement the waiver and the countermeasures the administration had taken to stop us. It was important that our documentation be indisputable and unimpeachable, and I was adamant that no opinions, speculations, or assumptions be included in the memos. This was not an easy task; it was often a challenge to avoid mixing subjective commentary with objective documentation. The administration's conduct had been egregious. We were writing about the callous dismantling of our agency and the obliteration of the progress we had made over our entire careers. Yet I insisted that we remove any content that was not directly backed by evidence, and that all conclusions and assertions be fully grounded in the facts that had transpired.

There was another problem. Julie was not on board with my plan to release the memos. She recognized the value of documenting the timeline of events that had led to the destruction of USAID, but she also believed that disclosing that documentation would only serve to further antagonize Mark, Tim, Joel, and the other political appointees whose actions—and especially inactions—were chronicled throughout the memos. She still believed that we could save some portion of our programs by cooperating with the political appointees, by getting in their good graces and earning their trust in order to convince them of the value of our work. She argued that the memos should not be sent out. Instead they should be saved internally for posterity—as a "memo to the file"—but not shared.

I desperately wanted Julie's sign-off on the memos. As acting assistant administrator, I technically outranked her at the moment, but Julie was unquestionably the most influential official in the bureau, and her opinions carried substantial weight among the staff. I wanted the memos to represent the unanimous consensus of GH, and that would not be possible without having Julie on board. But I was unwilling to compromise on the issues that Julie most fiercely resisted. I refused to remove the names of specific political appointees and DOGE team members who had prevented the implementation of lifesaving activities. And burying the memos in an internal file was not an option I was willing to consider. It was past time to speak out, and my mind was made up. I was resolved to make use of what was likely my last opportunity to expose the administration's lies, cruelty, and recklessness. I would release the memos with or without Julie's support.

22.

Click (Days 40–42)

On Friday, February 28, USAID designated several hours for former employees who had worked in the Reagan Building to retrieve their personal belongings. In rigidly assigned fifteen-minute time slots, individuals were permitted to enter the premises and take anything they could carry from their former workstations. As word spread that the ousted civil servants were being given one last opportunity to enter USAID headquarters, a crowd—comprised of former staff members and their families, foreign aid advocates, reporters, and curious passersby—began to gather outside the building's entrance. The growing crowd cheered loudly each time a former USAIDer exited, carrying all that remained of their public service careers in cardboard boxes and tote bags.

When news of the "clap out" reached the remaining USAID contingent in our new office on 12th Street, a large group of my GH colleagues decided to walk over to the Reagan Building to stand in solidarity with our former colleagues. Coincidentally, that morning someone had uncovered a trove of USAID-branded clothing in a supply room in the 12th Street office—utility vests, caps, and shirts that were usually worn overseas during crises to easily identify the U.S. government's emergency first responders, known as Disaster Assistance Response Teams (DARTs), who were delivering lifesaving aid. But with the Trump administration's cuts, USAID's DARTs were now obsolete, so the iconic clothing—recognized around the world as a symbol of American generosity and goodwill—was now offered up as keepsakes and memorabilia of a bygone era.

Around 1 p.m., a few dozen GH staffers and I decked ourselves out in the discarded DART clothes and set out on the ten-minute walk to the Reagan Building, to spend our lunch break celebrating the careers of our forsaken colleagues. As we made our way out of the elevators, we walked right past Mark, Tim, Ken, and a few other USAID political appointees. They were heading back up to their offices, presumably from meetings that morning at the State Department to finalize the drawdown of USAID. Their pressed suits and stern faces were a stark contrast to our ill-fitting matching outfits, and we were unable to stifle our giggles. We were feeling slightly rebellious, or maybe it was just that we didn't have much left to lose. One of my colleagues flashed a mock salute to the passing political appointees as they shuffled by trying to avoid eye contact with us, and then we exited the building into the early-afternoon sunshine.

When we arrived at the Reagan Building, a powerful surge of emotion swept over me. It was heartening to see the large crowd that had gathered to support the departing USAID employees, and to see familiar faces among those who were leaving the building. It felt satisfying simply to whistle and clap in recognition of the esteemed careers of my former colleagues. But it was also extremely sad to see the people we were losing, whose service to the country had been reduced to a few items hastily thrown into a box as they were ushered out the door. It was devastating to consider that each person represented a program that had been saving or improving lives, programs that were no more.

Ultimately, it was the anger that crowded out my other emotions that afternoon. As I watched each former employee leave, I was enraged by how unfair and arbitrary it was that these experts in their fields were being forced out by a group of unqualified and vindictive political operatives who could never understand, much less replicate, the talent they were unceremoniously snuffing from the federal ranks. I was furious with Congress and the courts for sitting back and watching as DOGE and the USAID political appointees ravaged an agency that had been created by a congressional act. Most of all, I was angry with myself: I felt that I had failed to do everything in my power to prevent this travesty. I had not spoken up early enough, loudly enough.

At some point, the lump in my throat grew so large I thought I might choke. I slunk away from my colleagues, who continued to cheer on the exiting employees, and I finally let myself cry. My tears were the first I had shed in twenty-two years, since the morning I reached the summit of Kilimanjaro. But today, my tears were born of anger instead of triumph. Far from that mountaintop, I felt as if I were falling into an abyss.

After a minute or two, I pulled myself together and returned to the group. It was nearly time to head back to the 12th Street office, and I knew what needed to be done when we got there. We needed to finish those memos. I was ready to sign them and send them out.

The first two memos, the ones documenting the ways we had been prevented from implementing the waiver and the destruction of our workforce, were ready that Friday afternoon. After a few final tweaks, I signed them both and saved the signed versions in a shared network drive, accessible to anyone who still had network access, as a precaution in case I was placed on administrative leave before I got the chance to send them out. The third memo, the one warning of the risks of the cuts to public health and national security, was not yet quite complete. The analysis was ready, but I still needed to give it a final review to ensure that the conclusions were presented objectively and impartially. My plan was to submit this memo to USAID's political leadership before sending it out with the other two. Even though it was not yet signed, it was also saved in the shared drive, just in case.

I wanted to send out the memos together, but I knew I couldn't wait much longer. By now, I had made up my mind that I needed to get the facts out urgently. The memos idling on the USAID network, where anyone could read, copy, or delete them, felt like a vulnerability, and I wanted to send them out on my terms. By Friday afternoon, I noticed that the normal stream of emails from Mark, Tim, and Joel had stopped, and I had the foreboding sense that my time at USAID was growing short. I drafted a cover email to accompany the memos, populating the bcc line with the nearly eight hundred personal emails of every member of GH as of January 20. I kept the draft open in my inbox, ready to be sent at a moment's notice. If I were placed on administrative leave without warning, I reasoned, I might have only a brief window to hit send before losing access to my email account. If I'd even have that.

At the end of the day on Friday, I had a premonition that I would not be coming back to the office on Monday. I walked around the ninth floor, saying what felt like a final goodbye to my colleagues. I shared hugs with many of them, who seemed to share my sense that they wouldn't see me again the next week. Then I left the 12th Street office for the last time.

Jordanna and I spent that weekend in Richmond, Virginia, where our daughter, Hazel, had a soccer tournament. On the two-hour drive that Friday evening, we talked about what I should do. I wanted to make sure Jordanna was on board with me sending out the memos, even though it would likely cost me my job. She had known that the memos were nearly ready, but now it was decision time, and I didn't know if I could send them if she didn't agree. To my relief, Jordanna had no doubt that I needed to do the right thing.

"You're miserable there," she reminded me. "You've been miserable for weeks. Do you see any chance of things improving if you stay?"

I told her I didn't. I could only foresee several more weeks of grave digging until I was finally cast off.

"And if you send the memos?" she continued. "Do you think that would actually make a difference?"

"I don't know, maybe not," I said. "But at least I will have done *something*. If nothing else, it would be a warning to other agencies that might find themselves in the situation USAID's in now. Maybe they won't make the same mistakes we did. Plus, with Elon and Pete Marocco lying about what's going on at USAID, this is my last chance to set the record straight from inside the government. I think I owe that to my team."

Jordanna agreed, and she helped me frame the situation as an easy decision. "Even if you somehow were able to keep your job at USAID, what would you even be doing there now that all the programs have been terminated?" she asked. "Sure, it would be nice to keep your paycheck. But how much is that worth if you're always going to regret not speaking out when you had the chance?"

After that discussion, it was no longer a question of if, but when. I spent the weekend alternating between distractedly watching Hazel's soccer games, doing a final review of the memos, and taking Signal calls with Nida, Ramona, and Natalia. We were unanimous that we had exhausted all our other options; the only remaining issue was timing. I had my draft email ready and could send the memos right then, from the soccer field. But should we wait until the third memo was finalized? Did we want to make another push for Julie to sign on? If so, we could leave everything until Monday—but could we wait that long? We decided to hold off until Sunday afternoon, when I planned to return to Washington. I scheduled a videoconference call with Atul Gawande for 4 p.m. for us to talk through our plan with him and get his advice on timing.

Driving home on Sunday, March 2, I tried to comprehend how things had gotten to the point where I was about to send an email that would surely end my civil service career. By now, I was convinced that continuing to remain silent about what I had witnessed—and, to some degree, participated in—was tantamount to complicity. But it was hard to sacrifice the job I had loved, and I was a little scared about what would come next. I reminded myself that the work that had meant so much to me was already gone, and there was nothing else to lose. And once again I renewed the promise I had made to myself to not be intimidated. I knew what had to be done.

Nida, Ramona, and I spoke with Atul that afternoon. We described the memos and our plan for sharing them. Atul helped us think things through one last time.

"You understand the consequences of sending this, right?" he confirmed. "And your families are on board, too?" We all nodded. He reassured us that we were doing the right thing, the only thing left to do.

Then he helped us settle the timing issue with a simple question. "If you are put on administrative leave with no advance notice, are you *sure* that you'll have time to send out the memos before you're kicked off the system?" he asked me.

I considered this. I thought I would probably have a short window. In several cases, including when Julie and her colleagues had been placed on administrative leave on January 27, they'd had nearly thirty minutes after being notified before their email was shut down, which would leave plenty of time for me to act. But others had never received any notification, and had only learned that they'd been ousted after they had lost email access.

"No," I said. "I'm not one hundred percent sure."

"Then can you afford to wait any longer?" he prodded.

We could not. Nida, Ramona, and I agreed that I had to send the memos now.

We ended the call with Atul and walked through my cover email one more time, to make sure everything was exactly right. The third memo still was not finalized, so I couldn't send it officially. Instead, I shared the unsigned version with a small group of former GH officials who were ready to circulate it broadly as soon as I sent my email with the other two memos.

At 4:27 p.m., I saw an email land in my inbox, with the subject line "Notification of Administrative Leave." This was it, they were removing me. It was now or never.

Click.

It was done, the memos were out. Eight hundred current and former colleagues now had the documentation my team had compiled of the Trump administration's indifference and cruelty—and the impact on global health and national security of the reckless dismantling of USAID.

I sat at my desk, looking out my window as the late-winter sun began to set over the alley behind my house. I was calm; it was over. I did not feel brave. By the time I had clicked send, there was nothing else to do.

The calmness did not last long.

Within minutes, I received my first reply: "You are a patriot and a hero. Thank you." More than a hundred similar emails would land over the course of that evening. I was floored by the quick and overwhelming response. As I had anticipated, some of my former colleagues had forwarded my email, and the memos, including the third memo on the impact of the cuts, were spreading far and wide.

Within the hour, calls, texts, and emails started arriving from reporters. First *The Washington Post*, then *The New York Times*, Reuters, ProPublica, PBS, ABC, NBC, and a steady stream from the cable news networks. They were shocked by what the memos had disclosed. Now they wanted details, wanted me on their shows, wanted to hear why I had sent the memos, wanted a statement from the (soon-to-be-former) top global health official at USAID.

In a daze, I walked downstairs and was surprised to find my parents standing in our kitchen. My mother had decided to bake cookies for me to take into the office on Monday to share with my team, having heard that many of my colleagues had brought in donuts and pastries the previous week. She and my father had stopped by to deliver them. From the look of it, she must have been baking all weekend. They were holding plastic containers stuffed with what must have been hundreds of cookies.

I broke the news to my parents that I wouldn't be able to bring the cookies to my colleagues, that I had just been placed on administrative leave and would not be going back to the office at all.

"Oh no," my father said. "This happened just now?"

Then I showed them the story *The Washington Post* had posted minutes earlier, headlined "Senior USAID Official Ousted as He Details Problems Providing Lifesaving Aid."

"I'm so sorry," my mother said after reading the article. She hugged me tight, and then asked, "What are you going to do now?"

This was something I had not yet considered.

"I don't know," I said. I thought for a moment and then said it again. "I don't know. What are any of us going to do now?"

Epilogue

I spent the next four months on administrative leave, until I was formally terminated on July 1, 2025, the same day that the final remnants of USAID were officially shuttered. No longer allowed to do the job I was still being paid for, I turned my attention to two institutions that had the power to roll back the destruction of USAID, or at least to minimize the damage: Congress and the courts. But first I needed to adjust to a new reality.

When I sent the memos, I had been totally unprepared for the immediate fallout. For the previous several weeks, I had been singularly focused on my team's futile efforts to restart USAID's lifesaving programs, unaware of the extent to which the agency had become a political lightning rod and had captured the attention of the national media. Only a few weeks earlier, most Americans would have been hard-pressed to say what USAID was, but the image of Elon Musk putting American foreign aid into the wood chipper had galvanized much of the public, leading to protests across all fifty states against the agency's destruction. As Bill Gates put it: "The picture of the world's richest man killing the world's poorest children is not a pretty one." But to another broad swath of America, the dismantling of USAID was celebrated as a righteous triumph over a shadowy "criminal organization" that was wasting taxpayer dollars on "evil" schemes to undermine President Trump's agenda.

I was taken aback by how quickly my memos spread and how much coverage they received. Following the piece in *The Washington Post* on

March 2, *The New York Times* published its own article within hours, titled "USAID Memos Detail Human Costs of Cuts to Foreign Aid." The next morning, in response to an outpouring of inquiries from readers for more details, the *Times* followed up with a post titled simply "Read the Memo," which published in full my memo on the impacts of the cuts on global health. Within a day, most other major national and international news outlets had published their own articles, and my name was trending across social media platforms.

Overwhelmed by the response, I initially shied away from the unexpected media deluge, turning down invitations from CNN and MSNBC to appear on nearly a dozen nightly news shows, and declining reporters' requests for comment. I had been disheartened and appalled by the Trump administration's actions, but I was still a civil servant, not an activist. I was afraid that talking to Rachel Maddow or Anderson Cooper on national television might undercut the evidence-based appraisal my team had produced. I wanted to let the memos speak for themselves.

At the same time, though, I had no plans to keep quiet. As soon as I was relieved of duty, I started to look for opportunities to share information in ways that might be useful to combat or at least reduce the damage of the administration's actions. I knew there were several ongoing lawsuits to fight the dismantling of USAID, and I wanted to tell my story to any members of Congress who were willing to listen. But those first few days felt like drinking from a fire hose; my phone and email were exploding with offers from people claiming to be lawyers or advocates, in addition to the reporters I was trying to steer clear of.

Luckily, I had a lot of help. Within days of landing on administrative leave, I was connected with a highly organized support network of former USAID staff members who were already on administrative leave or had been fired. It should have come as no surprise that my dedicated former colleagues had not given up their efforts to preserve foreign aid just because they had been kicked out of the agency. I learned from them that it had been no accident that my memos had spread so quickly; the network they had created was geared up to share information like this. Now that I was out, they quickly put me in touch with lawyers representing the various plaintiffs suing the government over the dismantling of USAID, as well as with key contacts on Capitol Hill. They also offered resources to help protect myself and my family at a time when my head was spinning and strangers (who had somehow tracked down my home address) were showing up at my front door. They helped me connect with Whistleblower Aid, a nonprofit legal organization to support and protect whistleblowers, who generously offered to represent me on a pro bono basis.

With the help of Whistleblower Aid, I filed a disclosure to Congress and the independent Office of Special Counsel to formalize the content I had revealed in the memos. I filed affidavits in support of lawsuits against the administration's efforts to dismantle USAID. My first affidavit, along with the memos, was cited in a U.S. Supreme Court decision requiring USAID to pay its contractors approximately $2 billion for services they had already performed.

My primary motivation during my first few weeks on administrative leave was to reverse some of the damage that had been done, and my memos, and the attention they garnered, had contributed to some immediate success on that front. In the first week after I sent the memos, USAID "unterminated" approximately four hundred of the contracts they had canceled.

By revealing publicly how USAID had been actively prevented from saving lives, I aimed to use the facts and the details my team had documented to counter the erroneous and sinister arguments the administration was using to try to justify its decision to shred the agency. In testimony to the House Foreign Affairs Committee, Secretary of State Marco Rubio falsely proclaimed that "no one has died" as a result of the cuts to USAID. In response to the details in my memos showing that lifesaving humanitarian assistance had not been restarted, Pete Marocco tried to lay the blame for all delays on USAID's career staff. During a closed-door meeting with the Senate Foreign Relations Committee, Senator Jeanne Shaheen, the ranking Democrat on the committee, pushed Marocco to explain why hundreds of USAID programs that provided lifesaving services had been stopped if the administration was committed to allowing lifesaving assistance to continue. Marocco responded by brazenly suggesting to a hearing room full of U.S. senators that any failure to resume lifesaving activities was the result of "malicious compliance" by the USAID career staff, who were "self-imposing stop-work orders" on lifesaving activities. He also stated falsely that he had approved the continuation of all lifesaving humanitarian assistance. And so, his twisted assertion concluded, if any activities were not moving, that was due to insubordination by civil servants who were conspiring to undermine the administration.

Marocco's suggestion that career health experts who had dedicated their lives to improving global health would intentionally fail to implement lifesaving programs just to make the administration look bad was infuriating and ludicrous. But it provided a helpful window into the cynicism and disdain that colored the administration's view of the federal workforce.

The administration also claimed that dismantling USAID was an example of eliminating government waste. Elon Musk continued to point to DOGE's "Wall of Receipts" as evidence of all the money DOGE was saving American taxpayers by canceling contracts at USAID and other agencies. Leaving aside the faulty accounting that was heavily inflating these claims of savings—DOGE took credit for terminating contracts that had already ended or for which most or all of the funds had already been spent—DOGE's calculations relied on the false assumption that there was zero value in our investments in strengthening health systems and combating the spread of diseases.

DOGE's "savings" also failed to take into account the immense costs they were foisting on American taxpayers. By dismantling USAID's robust financial system, the administration incurred hundreds of millions of dollars of unnecessary costs, through mistakes—including several instances of sending payments to the wrong partners and massive overpayments to some contractors—and unprecedented levels of interest accrued on unpaid bills. Behind closed doors the administration admitted that its actions were actually racking up enormous bills. In an internal memo from June 2025, Jeremy Lewin estimated that the cost of closing USAID would exceed

$6 billion in unanticipated expenses, including hundreds of millions of dollars to resolve legal claims from terminated contractors and agency staff.

Determined to counter the baseless claims and accusations coming from the Trump administration, I met privately with members of Congress and their staff, Democrats and Republicans alike, and testified publicly to the House Foreign Affairs Committee and the Senate Foreign Relations Committee to further document the actions the administration had taken to destroy USAID, and the impact of these actions on lives around the world. I was grateful for the opportunity to share my testimony with the lawmakers who were empowered to hold executive branch officials accountable for administering foreign aid as Congress directed, and for preventing the destruction of a federal agency that Congress had established by law.

Unfortunately, despite thanking me repeatedly for my bravery and integrity in laying bare the administration's illegitimate and reckless actions, Congress failed to act. After the initial progress of reinstating a small percentage of the contracts that had been terminated, my efforts failed to contribute any further toward preserving USAID or its lifesaving work.

As much as I was determined to expose the malfeasance that had led to USAID's downfall, I had a burning case of FOMO, starting the day I was placed on administrative leave. I knew, of course, that the situation at USAID had become hopeless, and I was relieved to have finally spoken out against the indifference and cruelty of the administration. Still, I felt an unexpected twinge of jealousy toward my colleagues who continued to go into the office each day and remained in the fight to save America's global health programs.

Only Nida Parks and I had been placed on administrative leave on March 2, and Julie Wallace quickly assumed the unofficial role of leader of GH upon my removal. She continued to believe that USAID's programs could still be salvaged through strategic engagement with the agency's political appointees, and she saw my memos as counterproductive to that goal. From her perspective, they were far from heroic; they had made her job more difficult. On that Sunday night she called Mark Lloyd to try to distance herself from me and the memos. The next day, Natalia Machuca and Ramona Godbole went into the office not knowing what to expect. They had naturally assumed that they would also be placed on administrative leave, as their names had been listed as "drafters" on the memos I had sent.

Julie met with the entire GH team on Monday, March 3. She told them that I had gone rogue by releasing the memos and that I had failed "to take the long view." If anything, my memos had set back the chances of preserving USAID's global health programs. She made clear that further disclosures from inside USAID would not be productive and would not be tolerated. She intended to repair whatever damage I had done to GH's relationship with Mark Lloyd and reminded everyone that they were "here to serve." She pulled aside Natalia and Ramona and offered to help them evade retaliation for their parts in the memos, on the implicit condition that they fall in line with her leadership approach.

Many of the remaining staff at GH now gave Natalia and Ramona the cold shoulder, avoided talking to them in the office, and sometimes refused to make eye contact. Whether this was because they were unhappy about the release of the memos or afraid to be associated with the troublemakers, the effect was chilling. There were a few, however, who gave them knowing winks or quietly thanked them for writing the memos when no one else was within earshot. In the following weeks, Julie made occasional requests for my two former colleagues to make an effort to contribute to a positive work environment by emulating her upbeat disposition. Ultimately, Natalia, Ramona, and a few others who continued to voice their concerns about the "future state" of GH were moved to administrative leave in early April.

Julie and the shrinking GH team focused on completing the foreign assistance review to make recommendations on the future needs for global health programming. Following Julie's proposal from a few weeks earlier, with which I had strongly disagreed, GH's final recommendations included the termination of more than thirty additional contracts in exchange for reinstating several contracts that had previously been terminated. Julie was convinced that trying to justify all our lifesaving work was unlikely to succeed, and so she gambled instead that GH's best chance to reinstate some of the critical contracts was to offer up a slate of other USAID contracts to be sacrificed in their place.

To some degree, it turned out that both of us were right—and wrong. Some, but not all, of the contracts Julie had requested for reinstatement were "unterminated," while all the contracts she recommended for termination were canceled. However, as I had feared, the administration used Julie's recommendations not only to justify terminating the additional contracts but also as a legal defense in court against claims that they were terminating contracts arbitrarily and without authority.

Now, thanks to GH's recommendations, USAID's political leadership could make the legal argument that they had terminated the contracts because career officials at the agency had asked them to do so and had told them that the terminations were necessary to achieve America's global health objectives. Jeremy Lewin, who in mid-March was designated deputy administrator of USAID, used the GH recommendations as legal cover to justify his actions of terminating global health contracts in a sworn statement in federal court:

> The responsible administration of USAID's critical and lifesaving Global Health activities, including the PEPFAR HIV relief program, requires the termination or modification of certain existing grants or contracts in order to better allocate resources to higher-impact activities. One of my primary goals in assuming my delegated role is to secure the effective delivery of the PEPFAR program and to ensure that USAID's critical global health supply chain remains intact. To that end, I have reviewed requests from career staff to terminate certain unnecessary contracts in order to create room to reactivate, renegotiate, and sign new contracts with greater impact. I intend to timely approve many of these requests, which I have been advised are essential to ensure that millions of people living with HIV can timely receive their medication.

————

It was not long before reports began to emerge of the heartbreaking human toll taken by the abrupt termination of USAID's global health programs. In the weeks and months following my ouster, journalists and researchers had traveled the world to document the ramifications of the cuts for people and communities.

In response to Rubio's assertion that "no one has died," the *New York Times* columnist Nicholas Kristof depicted the carnage caused by the shuttering of USAID, which he witnessed during trips to South Sudan, Kenya, Uganda, the Democratic Republic of the Congo, Sierra Leone, and Liberia. Kristof described how the shuttering of USAID-funded clinics, the shortages of lifesaving medications and mosquito nets, and the firing of community health workers and ambulance drivers contributed to suffering and death among vulnerable populations. *The Washington Post* reported on the innumerable deaths in more than forty countries that were caused by the administration's failure to restart lifesaving USAID programs, which resulted in substantial delays in the delivery of hundreds of millions of dollars' worth of medications for HIV, tuberculosis, and malaria. The reporting recounted in harrowing detail how the cuts forced clinicians to make impossible decisions about who would receive the now-scarce lifesaving medications and who would not; how patients tried to ration their drugs when supplies ran out, only to become progressively sicker; and how parents lost children to diseases because they were unable to access services that USAID had, until recently, ensured were readily available.

Scores of similar reports were published cataloging the local impacts around the world. Much of the reporting on the suffering could only convey individual examples because the cuts to USAID's data monitoring and evaluation programs made it more difficult not only to track the prevalence of diseases but also to analyze the true impacts of the cuts to foreign aid.

However, some researchers began to get a sense of the scale of the devastation, confirming the impacts that I had forecasted in my memo. In a study published in June 2025 in *The Lancet*, a comprehensive forecasting analysis estimated the impacts of the cuts to USAID on mortality in low- and middle-income countries by 2030. The findings were staggering. If not reversed, the study concluded, the dismantling of USAID will in five years result in 14 million unnecessary deaths, including 4.5 million children under the age of five. Researchers at Boston University developed an impact counter to model and track the deaths that occurred due to the slashing of USAID programs. By February 2026, the impact counter estimated that more than 800,000 people, including more than 500,000 children, had already died worldwide as a consequence of the cuts to USAID's programs.

As the first signs of these impacts became clear, USAID was formally eliminated as a federal agency in July 2025, with only a tiny closeout team remaining through September. At the same time, the State Department scrambled to restart some of USAID's programs, rehiring a handful of experts who had worked in GH to reconstitute a vastly scaled-back global health portfolio. The meager team includes only two advisors for tuberculosis, the world's top infectious disease killer, down from a former team of thirty experts at USAID, who had managed a $400 million program that spanned twenty-four countries and contributed to saving tens of millions of lives.

This new skeleton crew at the State Department represents the last hope for American foreign aid to ameliorate the worst of the anticipated impacts from the termination of USAID and its programs, though it remains unclear whether they will be empowered with the resources and capacity to face the enormous challenges ahead. The elimination of USAID buried what little remains of foreign aid within the State Department's larger bureaucratic structure, representing a significant step backward from President Kennedy's plan—and Congress's legislation—to advance international development as a primary pillar of U.S. foreign policy. While the State Department has indicated its intent to continue to provide humanitarian assistance on a limited basis, it simultaneously signaled an end to USAID's approach of strengthening local systems for sustainable international development.

I have learned that the importance of my decision to document what happened at USAID extended beyond speaking up for the people in other countries whose lives depended on our agency's work. The chaos unfolding at USAID was coming for many other federal agencies as well. We had the unfortunate distinction of being the first agency on DOGE's hit list, but the callousness, dishonesty, and ineptitude we experienced offered a preview of how the rest of the Trump presidency was likely to unspool. The story of USAID's destruction is important because saving lives matters, but also as a symbol of where this administration was heading. They used USAID to build a manual to which they have referred repeatedly to decimate other federal agencies:

Step 1: Fabricate and spread false stories of waste and abuse to turn public opinion against the work the agency is doing.

Step 2: Infiltrate and immobilize IT and financial systems to prevent the provision of services.

Step 3: Terminate contracts to ensure that the damage cannot be reversed.

Step 4: Vilify, demoralize, and ultimately eliminate the staff.

Rinse. Repeat. The longer I stayed quiet about how this process unfolded at USAID, the easier it was for them to replicate it elsewhere.

In the ensuing months, many federal employees reached out to me from an array of departments and agencies where they had witnessed or been directed to implement illegal, unethical, destructive, and wasteful actions. They had seen my memos and came to me with questions about the process and consequences of becoming a whistleblower. I helped them weigh their options, talking them through the risks and benefits of speaking out to publicize the malfeasance versus trying to work within their structures to make improvements. Some ultimately became whistleblowers, while others are compiling documentation and may blow the whistle soon. Still others have decided that this was not the right course of action for them.

I know many other civil servants are out there right now who are grappling with similar issues, whether it is a team of tech operatives working to dismantle their agency's systems and contracts or political leadership upending rules and structures to undermine the legal functions of their department. They find themselves in the unenviable position of having to decide how to respond to the destructive misuse of power, even as their careers and livelihoods hang in the balance. It is with these individuals in mind that I share a few of the lessons I learned during the dismantling of USAID, lessons I wish I had learned and heeded earlier in my own journey.

1. *Make sure everything is in writing.* Insist that all orders, especially questionable ones, are issued in writing, with clear authority, before you act on them. This may result in illegitimate demands being withdrawn.

2. *Insist on educating leadership on your functions.* Find ways to convey to political leadership—in writing—the vital importance of your programs before they begin making cuts.

3. *Reaffirm your oath of office.* Identify in advance which orders align with your oath to faithfully execute your duties within the bounds of the law, and which orders would require you to act illegally or unethically—orders that violate statutes, regulations, appropriations law, or civil service protections, and those that compromise program integrity, public health or safety, or misuse of funds—and then refuse the latter, no matter the cost.

4. *Ask questions and seek clarification.* When orders are ambiguous or open to interpretation, always take the time to ask clarifying questions before acting—again, in writing—even when urgency seems to demand immediate action.

5. *Document and save everything.* Create detailed, contemporaneous memos documenting every incident with supporting evidence and a clear timeline, and regularly back up all critical records to external storage in case you suddenly lose access to your email and government systems (as long as this is consistent with rules for handling classified and sensitive materials).

6. *Avoid isolation.* Keep lines of communication open with your

colleagues, and lean on trusted friends and family to help you make better decisions.

7. *Uphold nonpartisanship.* Rely on your expertise and maintain professional, apolitical allegiance to law, evidence, and ethics. Avoid being baited into partisan arguments.

8. *Use protected reporting channels.* If you are unable to find support internally, contact your agency's inspector general, the U.S. Office of Special Counsel, or congressional oversight committees to disclose malfeasance.

9. *Maintain your routines.* Get some fresh air when you can, don't forget to eat, and do the things that help keep your mind sharp.

10. *Don't wait for someone else to act.* Take responsibility for documenting and acting on what you are experiencing rather than hoping someone else will do it. Remember that following an unlawful order is not a defense, even if others comply with it. You are accountable for the actions you take, even under direction.

"Courage is contagious," says Andrew Bakaj, the lead counsel for my legal team at Whistleblower Aid. It is one of his favorite maxims, capturing his strong belief that one of the most important reasons for whistleblowers like me to come forward is to encourage others to speak up when they witness wrongdoing.

To this day, I do not consider releasing my memos an act of bravery. I had simply run out of options. But it gives me hope to know that my decision to send the memos has inspired many people to take their own brave actions to expose the illegitimate or dangerous malfeasance that they have experienced. In each instance, I am reminded that normal people make important choices every day.

Acknowledgments

This book began as an attempt to make sense of an experience that upended my professional life and shook my understanding of public service. It could not have been completed without the dedication, integrity, and courage of the thousands of public servants at USAID who served honorably during the darkest hours of the agency's history. Many of them endured great personal risk to uphold the last vestiges of USAID's mission. Even after being unfairly relieved of duty, so many of them have continued their efforts to address the world's inequities in new and amazing ways. Their example has sustained me when the path forward felt uncertain.

Thank you to my former colleagues, especially those who pushed back when they needed to, held the line, or simply showed up each day determined to serve. They shared memories, documents, and perspectives that helped me validate my experience and reconstruct everything that happened. There are far too many to thank individually, but I must single out a small group who stood with me each day, providing invaluable wisdom to help navigate the unthinkable. Nida Parks, Alyssa Jernigan, Natalia Machuca, and Ramona Godbole embodied the compassion, expertise, judgment, and moral clarity of the civil service at its best. They upheld their oath, and in doing so, ensured that I upheld mine.

In the days after my memos went public and I was placed on administrative leave, I received an outpouring of support, guidance, and resources from former colleagues and friends. Andrew Bakaj, Libby Liu, Naomi

Seligman, Lauren Smith, Alexis Posel, Kyle Gardiner, and the rest of the fearless team at Whistleblower Aid worked tirelessly to elevate my disclosures while protecting my rights as a whistleblower.

Atul Gawande, who provided me with invaluable advice and mentorship from the moment I called him on a desperate night in February, helped me recognize that my ultimate responsibility was to bear witness to USAID's destruction.

My agent, David Patterson, believed in this project from the outset, even before he realized he'd have to patiently shepherd me through the unfamiliar world of publishing. My publisher, Judy Clain, and the outstanding Summit team, including Josie Kals, Neha Rajbhandary, and Kevwe Okumakube, immediately recognized the urgency of bringing this story forward at a moment when speaking out against the Trump administration was becoming increasingly risky. And my exceptional editor, Paul Golob, literally taught me how to write a book as I wrote it. He never pulled his punches, and I'm fairly certain there isn't a paragraph in these pages that wasn't strengthened by his edits (aside from this one, for which he'd scold me for using a double negative).

A handful of old friends deserve special acknowledgment. Thank you to Alex Sturtevant, Ignacio De La Huerta, Kasim Te, Evan Gilbert, and Brennan Igoe, five of my closest high school friends, whose daily group text—an endless stream of debates, family updates, memes, and hard truths—was a constant lifeline of humor, honesty, and the kind of unwavering love that only comes from those who have known you nearly all your life. Adrian Elfersy, Michael Glick, and Noah Fox took it upon themselves to create welcome distractions for me when they noticed I was beginning to unravel. My Glover Park crew generously made themselves available to pick up an extra carpool shift or rush over for an emergency beer when I needed them. Thank you, dear friends.

I am deeply grateful to my family. My parents, Peggy and Peter, who supported me every step along the winding path that led me to USAID, have continued to encourage me following the collapse of the career I loved. My brother, David, helped me wade through the emotional chaos that followed my dismissal to discover the story that I needed to tell, and then gave me the confidence to write it. I could always count on my sister, Liza, to drop by and provide me with a needed laugh, and she provided insightful feedback on ways to make my story more accessible to "non-bureaucrats." My mother-in-law, Toni, not only provided the critical eye of a legal writing professor to help tighten my writing; she also ran an intensive Nana Camp for my kids when we learned over the summer that I had three months to write the manuscript.

My amazing children were on my mind pretty much constantly as I wrote. Zander and Hazel, thank you for growing into the kindest, smartest, and most entertaining people a dad could ever wish for. I'm eternally proud of you.

Finally, Jordanna, my partner, coach, cheerleader, therapist, my compass, and my first reader. Thank you for everything. Even as my future feels incredibly uncertain these days, I cling to the only thing I need to know: Wherever the world takes me, I'll be going there with you.